When Reality Shines

When Reality Shines

Susan L. Majette

James C. Winston
Publishing Company, Inc.

Trade Division of Winston-Derek Publishers Group, Inc.

TO SOW THE FALLOW SOIL

PUBLISHED BY JAMES C. WINSTON PUBLISHING COMPANY, INC.
Trade Division of Winston-Derek Publishers Group, Inc.
Nashville, Tennessee 37205

Library of Congress Catalog Card No: 94-61158
ISBN: 1-55523-723-1

Printed in the United States of America

To God,
the sustaining force of my life,
and to my family,
whose undying love and support
never faded, no matter how dim life looked.

Table of Contents

Preface

There is a special something within us all, every human being upon the face of the earth. Most of us know of numerous external forces which we believe have definite influences over our lives, but few of us are aware of an even stronger internal force. Some intentionally ignore it, blatantly refusing to acknowledge its presence; some accidentally overlook it, while others only tap into it periodically, allowing it to play a very small and minute part of their everyday existence. This presents a sad situation, for this internal force is undoubtedly of great importance.

It is the source from which all strength and power flows. It is that intangible, invisible, unexplainable resource that is always at our disposal—never fading nor subsiding. It remains constant, although we may sometimes waver. Commonly known as the *inner-self*, it is that hidden ability we all have to sustain our own lives. It is spunk. It is guts; it is where we go and what we pull on when all else around us seems to fail, weaken, and lose its substance. It is faith, love, and perseverance. It is determination, *self*-determination; *Kujichagulia*—the swahili word for the determination to do and to be all that one can be in spite of adversity and negativity, dim conditions or circumstances.

There are a multitude of theories rendered to support this idea and numerous incidents wherein it has worked for different individuals in many different circumstances. But the real question is, *Has it ever worked for you?* Have you as an individual, as your own person, gotten in touch with your inner-self and tapped into your source of inner strength and power?

For the new person in you, just discovering your new found spirituality. May you learn, grow, and develop from the shared knowledge and experiences on the pages that follow.

Introduction

Sometimes I hear a small voice in my head, or maybe it's in my heart; no, I'm not insane. Sometimes I listen, sometimes I don't. Nevertheless, whether I heed this voice or not, one thing I know for certain . . . it never lies. It ministers only the truth—a deep-rooted, steadfast, immovable truth that no one can deny. It warns as it attempts to protect me; it guides as it attempts to direct my footsteps, and it even convicts me when I am wrong. There is no doubt that this voice is not me talking to myself; for all too often it frequently disagrees with my thoughts, my ideas, and my desires. It falls in sync with the natural laws of the universe—those constant harmonious precepts of this world's creations—as it labors to include me in the plan.

The little voice talked to me quite a bit before I was stricken with lupus, but I was too busy concentrating on the visible, controllable aspects of life to pay much attention to what was being said. Unfortunately, I was under the blind misconception that earthly concerns and the current physical state were the full extent of life. I later realized that messages transmitted by way of our physical senses reveal only one facet of life. It has very little to do with the true substance of our overall existence; for this type of understanding is limited to the minuscule activity of our brains, minds that are said to operate at only approximately 10 percent of their total capacity.

As I began listening to this little voice, I discovered that its messages penetrated much deeper than that of any physical appearance or my general five senses. It was a deep, somewhat mysterious sensation which I could explain by no other means than simply a *feeling*. It wasn't until I developed a relationship with my Creator that I realized it was my spirit speaking to me. My limited mind can only relate to the present and future through past events, teachings, or experiences; however, my spirit is a much wiser and illuminated life force that can transcend time and space. It is not limited to the here and now of this world. It happened in biblical times with Ezekiel[1] and John[2], and it has happened to me. In my mind, that clearly explained why this little voice, my little voice, was so very right most of the time.

Has your little voice ever told you not to do something, not to go to some particular place, and you ignored that voice and did it anyway—only to discover the consequences to be nothing but negative? Maybe afterwards, with a somewhat pragmatic attitude, you admitted, "Something told me not to do that." Of course it is then too late; the damage has already been done. *Your spirit was speaking to you!*

I never really appreciated the true friendship of my spirit until I was forced to rely on it for survival during a very serious illness. It led me and guided me in a path which I knew not. It was multifaceted, not only in its duties, but also in the execution of those duties. It could and did work through, around, with, and in every given situation with a type of wisdom and awareness not known to man. Knowing my Creator, the creator of this universe, as I do now—being fully aware that He *is* a spirit, the Ultimate Spirit, and that those who communicate with Him must do so in spirit and in truth, I now understand why the vibes of my spirit were and still are so very accurate, so on target with any given situation or circumstance. That was the one part of me, the only part of me, that could make contact with the author, maker, and even designer of the universe of which I am a part. God's Spirit being all wise, all knowing, omnipresent, and omnipotent, communicating with my inner-most being, led my spirit to assist me, the whole me—mind, body, and soul—to live each moment, each day, a little and sometimes a whole lot better.

[1] Ezekiel 8:3

[2] Revelation 4:2

I soon came to realize that the spirit within oneself and its one-ness with the Supreme Spirit is the true essence of life. It not only motivates, but can actually cause circumstances to occur. If one's spirit is low, one's perception is apt to be bleak, one's behavior neg-ative, with unpleasant circumstances inevitably following. On the other hand, if one's spirit is high, he/she feels good about himself, has a positive attitude, ignites and gives off positive energy, attracts positive people, and creates positive circumstances followed by positive consequences. Once I became cognizant of the fact that this particular facet of my being held this much power, I was cer-tain that my spiritual self was *my* true essence of life.

1. Paths of Passage

It was a spring day in 1980, March 23 I believe, when my eyes were opened to my first out-of-body experience. Returning home from what would be the first of many hospital visits was a much welcomed relief. I hadn't felt very sick upon entering the hospital, experiencing only an unusual rash and pain in several joints, but I was no doubt very ill by the time I was released. The series of rigorous, painful tests made for nine days of pure agony, and I was discharged in long-lasting, excruciating pain from head to toe, with a diagnosis of a strange and peculiar disease termed *systemic lupus erythematosus*. There are only two pleasant memories that I can recall regarding the entire negative experience. One memory surrounds the environment I found myself in, and the other involved a situation I put myself in.

The decor of the room, my home for those nine days, was the first. It left nothing but pleasant memories in the recesses of my mind as I think back on its uniqueness. The colorful sheets, covered with the small flower-like pattern of orange, yellow, and lime green, kissed the tangerine walls in a combination that yielded a much more pleasant and cheerful atmosphere than the usual drabness which is found in most institutions. It was almost as if I was in a candy store, taking me back to childhood days of carefree living in fantasy lands. I simply loved it and the positive psychological effect it generated.

The other memory surrounded a much more intimate experience which I haphazardly put myself into. Fasting of any sort can put a strain on the human body, especially when one is ill-prepared mentally, physically, or spiritually, and I was ill-prepared on all three counts. Having never experienced a *fast* before in my life, I definitely was not ready for it, especially not in a situation wherein it was imposed upon me. *What! Go for days with no food? Days without liquids? No water, no soda?* I screamed to myself. *Surely these people must be crazy!* I was a sick woman. I needed my nourishment, especially when they were drawing blood from me two and three times a day. And where would I get the strength I needed to fight the severe pains that seemed to be increasing by the minute? Surely these people, the so-called intelligentsia, well-learned of our society, had gone berserk!

Nevertheless, with prayer, very little prayer, and a lot of perseverance, I made it. Then one morning, with no warning at all, one of the nurses informed me, "Today is your day."

"You are free to eat anything you please today, but today only," she said with a smile, adding, "but no liquids."

"No liquids?"

"No liquids," she reiterated in her most authoritative tone. "The kidney tests are extremely important. Now we wouldn't want to mess that up would we?" Her eyes made contact with mine.

"I guess not," I agreed reluctantly. Still something is better than nothing, I thought to myself.

I quickly phoned my girlfriend, the only real friend I had acquired in Cincinnati. Glad to hear from me, she immediately picked up on the desperation in my voice as I begged her to bring me something *good* to eat. I love spicy foods, and the request for barbecue ribs rolled off my lips before I knew it, almost as if it was a gut response. At that point, I wasn't exactly sure what had driven me to request such an extremely spicy dish, whether it was the stale smell of hospital food that seemed stuck in my nostrils or the fact that I had been forced to refrain from ingesting any food at all for what seemed like such a long time. Whatever the case or the cause, I was definitely ready for some hot, spicy ribs.

I was elated as I waited with anticipation for Jenny to arrive. I came to realize that a good friend is a jewel to treasure, and Jenny was that kind of a friend. It was as if she had been my guardian angel from the time I had arrived in Cincinnati. She had been there for me, looking out for me, understanding me, and she always seemed to take up the slack when I was down and out. As she entered the room, she was all bundled up from the winter cold, but with a huge smile on her face showing all thirty-two white ones. I excitedly responded to her entrance, "Look at you!"

Our spirits and minds united as we smiled at each other, glad to see one another and overjoyed that I was now allowed to eat anything. The radical nature in my soul danced as I realized we had succeeded in going against the system by sneaking food into the hospital.

My level of excitement heightened as the spicy aroma saturated the room, and I received a real sense of consolation as the smell of barbecue sauce filled my nostrils. Midwesterners have a certain way with beef, you know? That's their specialty, and I was all too ready and well overdue for my treat. I had never been a big meat eater, but this time I could hardly wait. You know, our minds play tricks on us when we've identified something we cannot or should not have; that seems to be the one thing we want most of all. For days I had been told I couldn't eat this and couldn't eat that; no food on Monday, a no-liquid diet on Tuesday, and again no food on Wednesday. But this was my day! I could eat whatever I wished, and that thought had consumed my mind the entire day as I waited for Jenny to arrive.

Before I knew it, I was sitting on the side of the bed, totally oblivious to the pain I was in and so glad to have my attention diverted, even if only for a moment! Noticing her shivering body I said in a questioning tone, "It must really be cold out?" I had forgotten there were eight inches of snow on the ground because my little world had not extended past the confines of the hospital room for the past few days, and those days seemed like an eternity.

Emphatically acknowledging my mental state, she appeased me by saying, "Girl, you just don't know!"

"Well, take off your coat, and let's see what's in the bag," I invited.

She willingly handed me the bag but said, "The coat stays on, girl. It's cold out there!"

We both smiled again as I took the bag from her icy hands. We laughed and joked as I lavishly licked the tasty barbecue sauce from my fingers covered with greasy spices. Then my countenance suddenly changed. Jenny noticed a wide-eyed expression on my face and immediately asked what was wrong. Being too preoccupied with my situation and too devastated by what I was experiencing to explain, I simply stared back at her. Watching me frantically fan my mouth, she soon succumbed to uncontrollable laughter. My brain had registered a severe burning sensation, almost as if I had just taken a spoonful of cayenne pepper. The strong pungency of my tasty desires had turned my mouth into a flaming inferno.

I reached for my bedside water pitcher only to discover it empty. Sheer panic set in as I remembered why it was empty. This was the day designated for no liquid intake! Sure, I had been permitted to eat whatever my little heart desired, but soda, juice, and yes, even water were forbidden. The kidney tests to be performed eliminated the possibility of allowing any liquid to flow down my digestive tract for an entire twenty-four hour period. What was I to do?

This was approximately the eighteenth hour into the test, and one small drink of water would have ruined the validity of the test, negating the entire previous eighteen hours of suffering. *I will have to start all over*, I thought. The human mind can quickly adapt to traumatic situations, and in my mind this registered as just such an instance.

My reflex mechanism kicked in, and I scurried to the bathroom, cupping my hand to receive one of God's most wonderful inventions. All the while, Jenny was still laughing and asking what was wrong, as if she didn't know. The water, cold as ice itself, made its way through the pipes to the faucet only to lightly brush at my fire. As I repeated the process of swishing and spitting, my tongue did receive a little relief, but my throat and entire digestive tract remained untouched. Just a few swallows would have made me feel as if I had plunged my entire body into a large pool of water on a hot summer's day, but wishing and hoping would be as close as I would get to the feeling of total relief and comfort. I could fantasize to my heart's content, but would in no way experience that type of relief in this situation. There was no way I was willing to forfeit the progress I had made thus far in completing the kidney test and subsequently have to start over again.

Unbeknownst to me at the time, I could have gotten away with it, but at this point my ultimate goal was to complete the series of tests so I could go home as soon as possible. I knew the burning sensation would diminish eventually, and it was entirely up to me to use the mind over matter technique to deal with the discomfort until it passed. Little did I know this would be just one of the many situations wherein it would be necessary for me to psych myself out to overlook the obvious and rise above my situation in order to deal.

Once the shock of what had happened was over and the towering inferno had been calmed to a flaming fire, I was able to tell Jenny all about the kidney test, the doctor's instructions, and the imaginary flames in my throat. Then and only then was I able to laugh with her as we soon both succumbed to uncontrollable outbursts. During this episode, I was much too blind to see that, as it is said, God takes care of babies and fools. My body was not up to handling a full meal of spices after fasting on and off during the previous days. It was a blessing in disguise that I couldn't finish the ribs. Jenny and I had weathered another calamitous situation. It was a very small catastrophe indeed, yet it served to leave us with one more noteworthy incident in the archives of our friendship.

The stage had been set for the nine-day hospital trauma by a succession of doctor visits, all for the purpose of finding the cause of the mysterious rash that, much to my dismay, seemed to be continuously spreading to new, untouched areas of my body. Although most of the doctors I visited had no idea what the problem was, they were honest, maybe a little too honest. I appreciated the candor, except when they would carelessly leave tact and sensitivity at the door. One doctor did just that; entered the examining room, looked at my frightened face as I lay on the examining table, and with a somewhat pensive look on his face said, "Looks like you have lupus." He then turned and walked out of the room never to return.

Maybe he's gone to get another piece of equipment, I thought, *or maybe an information pamphlet explaining this thing called* lupus. But that was a joke, and the joke was on me. He never did return. I waited and waited anxiously for an answer. I had been searching for months. Finally, a nurse reentered to prepare the room for the next patient. A bit disturbed, I asked, "Where is Dr. Cheeks?"

"Oh, he's in with another patient," she replied. I was appalled!

Feeling somewhat abandoned and wallowing in my own sorrowful self-pity, I responded to his inconsiderate behavior with anger, picked up my purse and left. *How could he make such a statement and just walk out of the room? Didn't he have any manners or consideration for other people, for me in particular? What is lupus, anyway? It must not be serious. What a waste of money! He'll never get any more of mine*, I thought to myself.

My normally assertive personality had been spent on the many trials up to this point, and I felt I was losing my fight. Choking back the tears, I drove home in the dusk of the evening in a complete daze, wondering what to do next. *This has been the fourth doctor*, I thought. *Still no answer. Still a progressing rash. As if that's not enough, now I seem to be losing my hair too! What in the world am I going to do? What do I do now?*

Once the anger subsided, logic stepped back in, and I realized I had to find out what was wrong with my health. Back to the yellow pages I went. "An appointment in a week? I can handle that, I guess," I replied to yet another new and professional-sounding voice on the other end of the telephone line. Working diligently to regain the optimism that had been such a real part of my personage in times past, I waited for the week to pass.

The new doctor readily explained that a skin biopsy of one of the lesions would no doubt give me the answers I so desperately searched for, all the while neglecting to inform me of the pain and permanent scar it would leave behind. He did inform me, though, that the test results would be back in a week.

OK, Susan, let's wait one more *week*, I consoled myself.

A week and two days passed. A week and five days passed; still no phone call from his office. I called him only to discover that he was on vacation in the islands. "He'll be back in two weeks," his secretary stated.

What is this, I thought; *does someone have it in for me?* Well, I couldn't wait two *more* weeks, so back to the yellow pages again to find another doctor. "Good . . . an appointment at the end of the week? That's great!" I exclaimed.

Those days I seemed to be a bundle of tears, nerves more than frazzled, and yet I was still expected to smile and perform at work. One day a co-worker noticed the rash and asked what was wrong. That was all I needed. My sudden burst of tears quickly answered her question more effectively than my words ever could. I had no idea of what was wrong; but I knew something definitely was, and that was exactly what my tears conveyed.

Sympathetic to my problem, she recommended her father's physician, one who she swore could work miracles because he helped her father's hair grow back when he started going bald. *That sounds like just the thing I need,* I thought to myself. So, desperate for an answer to my problem, I moved on with my quest. I took her advice, cancelled the appointment I had previously made with the unknown physician in the yellow pages, and made an appointment with Sharon's Dr. Robb.

This waiting period was the same nightmare as the other, like a sleepless night waiting for the dawn of a new day. But truly the dawn does follow the darkness, and the day of my appointment with this new physician finally arrived.

"Good evening, Ms. Majette. Dr. Robb will be with you shortly."

Umm, she seems nice, I thought. *What a pleasant change from the last doctor's office. No interest in magazines here,* I told myself, clarifying my priorities. *Let's just get on with the show!*

"Ms. Majette, Dr. Robb will see you now."

Having no understanding of the spirit realm at the time, I still realized something was different about the visit. Something felt good about his office; something simply felt good about being there. There was a peace about it. At that time I thought it was the music or the decor. Now I understand it was simply divine order in place. My spirit must have known I would end up at Dr. Robb's office and that this visit would start the ball rolling for all other events in my life.

As I sat on yet another examining table, I noticed the anxiety building as my mind's eye reflected back on the many other preceding doctors' visits. Just as I felt a wave of gloom approaching, I witnessed a short-statured, dark-haired, Italian gentleman enter the room. His warm, reassuring smile soon put me at ease as I began sharing the saga of my quest. Listening attentively until I finished, he then reaffirmed one of the other doctor's tentative diagnosis as he agreed, "It could very well be lupus. Why not let's call Dr. Cole's office for the test results of the skin biopsy?"

"You can do that?" I was surprised. Someone was finally on my side and was going to help me.

"Sure, just a minute," he said, and he departed from the room.

"Oh, great! I'm finally gonna get some answers," I said aloud to myself. I felt as if it was my birthday, and I was about to open the largest present ever.

I waited in a wave of conflicting emotions: anxiety, fear, skepticism, relief, optimism, and pessimism, all at once. All of these divergent feelings came crashing down like the waves of many waters. I waited for what seemed like forever, when Dr. Robb re-entered the room with the confirmation. "You *do* have lupus."

"*Lupus?*" I repeated in disbelief.

"Yes, lupus," he replied. "It's a blood disorder affecting the immune system of young women, usually of childbearing age," he attempted to explain.

I looked in complete silence and total amazement. *I've got some strange disease?* I thought to myself as he continued to explain.

". . . there is no known cure, but science has advanced a lot and we do have quite a bit of success in controlling it . . ." His voice faded in my ears, and the words jumbled themselves in my head as I began to feel numb all over.

I had waited so long, for months, to find out what was wrong with me, but I was in no way ready for this! Regaining composure, I struggled to ask, "What do we do now?" Yes, *we*, because I definitely needed help with this one. Not fully comprehending the severity of my new situation, I reasoned that this, like everything else, had an answer. According to my way of thinking, it was simple. You just look at the problem, decide what to do about it, act, and just as mysteriously as it arose, poof, it will disappear. Naive little me! As our conversation progressed, I began to realize that the answer, in this case, was not that simple at all. I wasn't even sure if there was an answer.

"Well, the first step is to check your organs to see if there has been any damage," he answered. "You'll need to see an internist."

"Sounds serious. I'm afraid," I confessed.

He comforted me by bringing me back to the reality of what we needed to do to address the situation. "Do you have a doctor here?"

"No", I replied. *Why should I have had a doctor when I had never been sick*, I thought to myself.

"There is an internist on the board of directors with me at Bethesda General who has had quite a bit of experience with lupus patients."

He paused for me to respond, maybe with even a tinge of excitement, or maybe just plain approval, or at least some relief. But I was much too shaken to do anything but simply sit, completely dumbfounded. Noting my mental state, he suggested, "Would you like my secretary to make an appointment for you?"

"Yes, please," my voice trembled.

As he left the room, I attempted to replay our conversation in my mind, but all I could hear ringing in my ears was *there is no cure*. Dr. Robb returned much sooner than I anticipated, or maybe my mind was so paralyzed that I misconstrued the true passage of time. He eagerly informed me of the date and time of my appointment with a Dr. Carmine, his colleague at Bethesda. Finally someone had acknowledged the urgency of my situation, and I was only asked to wait three more days. Thank God! Just days, not weeks. It's amazing how everything is relative, even the scope of time.

Still numb from the diagnosis, I went through the motions of politely thanking Dr. Robb and his staff for all of their help. I left the office, got in my car, and drove home, all in the same numb stupor, the same comatose state of mind. No doubt the angels of God guided me home that evening, even in the midst of my ignorance of their existence.

In the comfortable confines of my one-bedroom apartment, cozy and stylishly decorated with contemporary furnishings, exposed brick walls and warm fireplaces, I sat quietly, experiencing the first small sense of relief I'd had in months. I finally had some answers regarding what was wrong with me, what I needed to do to correct the situation, and where to go from there. Although, the newfound information I had received only minutes before now shed a whole new light on the reality of my life. It was now being threatened! Not my job, not my finances, not even my love life, but my actual existence was now threatened. "Is this really real?" I asked. "It can't be! I'm too young," I protested. "I have too much going for myself. I'm just beginning to taste life, to stand on my own two feet. I'm going places, meeting people, doing new things. Surely it can't be as serious as Dr. Robb made it sound!" I argued.

Determined to find evidence to substantiate my arguments, I quickly rose and ran to my bedroom, sure that the Webster's dictionary on the shelf would establish my stand and confirm my hopes that surely this disease was in no way a very serious one.

As I fumbled through the pages, I could feel my heart racing and thumping with excitement. There it was in bold print, *lupus erythematosus*, and it read, ". . . a slowly progressive systemic disease that is marked by degenerative changes of collagenous tissues with erythematous skin lesions, arthritic changes, lesions of internal organs, and wasting, and by even leukemia and endocarditis." What in the world was this monster that was supposed to be a part of my life, which was threatening to take over my life, and which might possibly destroy my life?

Not having the knowledge of medical terminology that I have today, there was a lot I did not understand; however, I did understand the word *degenerative*. In my dictionary that meant *continuously worsening*. My eyes hurriedly skimmed over the other words, and they froze on the word *wasting*; was I going to waste away? And Oh, my God! Leukemia! That alone could kill you; I had an uncle who died from that! The truth had now registered in my brain. *I was going to die.*

Before the tears could well up in my eyes, I had broken out in uncontrollable sobs, sobs so loud that my neighbor came knocking at my door. I ran to the door, not knowing or even caring who was there. All I knew, deep down on the inside, as well as on the surface of my consciousness, was that I needed someone, anyone, as long as it was another human being with whom I could share my shocking news.

As I opened the door, still in sobs, my tearful eyes met Jim's face, filled with concern as he asked, "What's wrong with you? I heard you crying all the way next door!" I calmed myself down enough to explain, showing him what Mr. Webster had stated. Taught to value man's education, I truly believed Webster's dictionary as the absolute truth, so there was no possibility of fallacy. He tried to console me, but what does one say to a hysterical friend who has just discovered she has a fatal illness when both are so young and inexperienced with life?

Time stood still until there were no more tears left to even trickle down my cheeks. I sat, comatose again, as my emotional roller coaster came to a screeching halt. First the anxiety and confusion of not knowing, then the relief of knowing, followed by shock and hurt and more confusion; all in the same day, after weeks of uncertainties. I was left with an overwhelming feeling of just plain fear, which simply left me numb all over again. *OK, Susan, pull it together! You have to deal; you must deal! Back to logic here,* I told myself. *You'll go to the doctor in a few days, and you'll know more then. Anyway, you're not dead yet, so just go on with life.* The dictionary said degenerative. *That in itself indicates you have some time,* I told myself, as I tried to rationalize my situation. Sure, go on with life; continue with the job and life as usual.

Well, I tried, but the sales calls didn't seem to matter anymore, nor were they successful. The stiffness in my legs increased. My first thought was that it was strictly psychological; I knew I had been diagnosed with this illness, and so I thought I was imagining having the symptoms. Later, I found that stress sometimes heightens the disease activity of lupus. I had definitely been stressed out, so the increased stiffness was real.

The days dragged on until the date of my appointment with the internist finally arrived. Dr. Carmine was a calm, pleasant looking gentleman in his mid fifties. His office was small and modest, appearing to have once been someone's home, now converted into an office. The waiting room must have once been the living room, and his personal office appeared to have been the dining room. The upstairs bedrooms had been converted into examining rooms, including the third floor. All of the examining equipment seemed to be obsolete—that old-fashioned, snow-white enamel that used to be around when I was a kid; it appeared to be the original stuff left over from the 1950s.

The old cliche, *don't judge a book by its cover*, was more than appropriate here because Dr. Carmine was anything but obsolete. He turned out to be one of the most innovative, skillful, and knowledgeable doctors I have ever met. He was a practical man in all respects. That explained why he still used such out-dated furnishings, for they were still very much in operable condition. I was young, flamboyant, idealistic, and a little ignorant, but I soon learned.

As he approached me with his pleasant smile and joking manner, he formally introduced himself. He then gave me a brief spiel about Dr. Robb's phone call and the lab findings from the biopsy report. After down-playing the theatrics of an incurable disease, while simultaneously being honest about its seriousness, he politely asked, "Now, do you have any questions?"

I sat there quietly the entire time, listening very closely to his every word, utilizing my psychology background from college whenever possible, detecting his careful choice of words and sentences designed to try to keep me calm. While I appeared to be calm on the outside, I felt like a reservoir of mighty rushing waters on the inside, just waiting to break loose and held back only by my dam of silence. But now the time had come to break that silence, to burst the dam of protection.

Although I opened my mouth with the total intent of asking a very intelligent question, the direct opposite occurred. My question was not an intelligent one at all, but instead strictly an emotional response. My manner was no longer quiet nor controlled, but instead, violently unruly. The pent-up anxiety and suppressed fears I had been harboring for days were at the threshold of being released. I was so excited to reach the *grand wizard*, the man with all the answers, that all couth just flew out of the window. My fears and anxieties were voiced in one huge outbreak of sobs, flooded with tears pretty much like the ones I had experienced in my living room that evening after my visit with Dr. Robb. Then the most important words I had ever spoken in my life squeezed themselves out through the wails of my cry; I asked, "Am I going to die?"

Dr. Carmine looked stunned for a moment, probably because of the false impression of calmness I had portrayed from the time we met. Here was what had appeared to be a very calm, cool, collected, bright young woman doing an about face on him and, in no time at all, simply bugging out. His surprise at my outburst lasted only a brief moment, and Dr. Carmine quickly regained his composure. Understanding my distress, in a sympathetic voice coupled with his reassuring smile, he replied, "No, of course not."

Although his answer was exactly what I both wanted and needed to hear, I continued to cry uncontrollable tears, but this time they were tears of relief. He handed me a few tissues from the box atop his paper-filled desk, rose out of his easy chair, and said rather emphatically, "Get yourself together. I'll be right back."

After a while, the tears stopped. Then my mind began to talk to me. *Is he really telling me the truth*, I wondered. *Does he really know what he's talking about? Well, he is the doctor. But then look at what kind of doctors I have been running into lately. He could be a quack, too! His office is mighty small*, my mind continued with it's logical song and dance. You know how we can talk ourselves into or out of just about anything.

Before I could decide whether I should trust him or not, he was back in the room. "Well, that's better," he said, responding to the drying of my tear ducts. "Now, the first thing we need to do is find out exactly what's going on. So we need to put you in the hospital and run some tests."

That sounded simple enough to me. I has only been admitted to the hospital once before in my entire life. That was when I had my tonsils removed as a child, but I'd heard that's what they do to people when they need to find out what's wrong with them; they put them in the hospital and run some tests. *At least it seems to be a step in the right direction*, I thought to myself.

I apologized to Dr. Carmine for my irrational behavior, although it wasn't really irrational to me. I had just been diagnosed with an incurable disease, almost like AIDS. I just thought apologizing was the right thing to do. Dr. Carmine understood completely, even without any explanation on my part. We both smiled and shook hands on what was beginning to develop into a very special doctor–patient friendship.

I phoned Mom to let her know of the progress in my search to find out what was wrong with my health. "He says I need to go in the hospital to have some tests done," I explained.

Aware of how important this was and knowing how desperate we both were to find answers, she simply asked, "When are you going in?"

"Day after tomorrow. I have to get some things straight first." With little pause and even less hesitancy, I anxiously asked, "You are coming, aren't you?" Boy did I need support! The tone of my voice heightened with my anticipation of her answer, unsaid yet very obvious; getting her there was one of the things I had to get straightened out.

Loving me, and needing to be there just as much as I loved her and needed her to be there, she responded with no hesitation and very much conviction, "Sure! You know I will." And after briefly discussing with me a few of my fears, she closed the conversation with, "I'll call you right back as soon as I get the bus schedule."

A few minutes later, the phone rang, and she informed me of her expected time of arrival the next day. She also notified me that Aunt Evelyn, I jokingly call her *Johnny on the spot*, would be coming, also. Although her stay would be somewhat brief, Aunt Evelyn was one of those always-ready-to-lend-a-hand types of relatives, and I was glad she was coming.

Arriving safely as expected, Mom spotted me across the bus station lobby, all bundled in my black winter hat and coat, attempting to brave the February cold of the Midwest. It wasn't until months later that she confided in me the pain and anguish she felt when her eyes first made contact with my inflamed face, beet red and full of sores. She tried to hide her emotions, but her devastation was obvious to me. We just didn't discuss it. We had been in very close contact during my many trials since arriving in Cincinnati; I had kept her abreast of my physical problems, but seeing firsthand what was happening really put things in a whole new perspective for her. The next day we made the necessary preparations, and off to the first phase of my crisis we went, straight to Bethesda General Hospital.

Soon, I found myself confined to the four walls of what was to be my temporary dwelling place, surrounded by strangers, a funny smell, and cheerful decor. I was a little apprehensive at first, but my preoccupation with what *could* happen was soon bombarded with the realities of what *was* happening.

The needles, syringes, tubes, charts, and electronic equipment quickly multiplied in number and frequency as one test ended and another began. Although different in some respects, the scenes were still very similar; poking, sticking, stabbing, and jabbing seemed to be the name of the game. Whether it was my heart, lungs, kidneys, or liver being evaluated, my role was always the same; just grin and bear it. Whether they were shooting dye into my veins or taking one of the sets of seven vials of blood, which they did with clockwork regularity at 6:00 A.M., 3:00 P.M., and 9:00 P.M. each day, my role remained the same; grin and bear it.

I had no real problem grinning and bearing it at first; even my questions were few. I only wondered: *Why did they have to disturb my sleep in the wee hours of the morning; didn't they know it's hard to be courageous when woken out of your sleep?* and *If God knew I would be stuck this much intravenously, why didn't He give me more than one good vein?*

Although the tests were a pain, in more ways than one, the preparations for them were even worse. Foods and liquids have a tendency to really interfere with the validity of tests, so I was told. So that seemed to be the overall concern of the medical staff when preparing me or, I should say, preparing my body for the tests they wanted to perform. I say my body because, after a while, I got the impression that they didn't seem to care much at all that there was a real person inside.

Being required to omit food on some days and all liquids including water on others seemed a little extreme to me at first. But the real cruel and seemingly unnecessary act of preparation came when they started giving me this black gook called *X-Prep* almost everyday. X-Prep is a very strong laxative. It's black and thick and aimed at cleansing the upper and lower intestines. I understood fully what the laxative was supposed to do. I even understood why I needed to have it done. I just couldn't understand why I was given such a harsh laxative so frequently, every other day as a matter of fact, when I had been given no food at all! And why didn't anyone care enough to give patients like me, undergoing such brutal treatment, some Charmin? These are the questions I would ask myself each of the many times I was forced to go to the bathroom.

Still, my part was the same; simply grin and bear it. I played my part very well, I thought, until the very last test. I'm still not sure whether the doctor saved the most horrendous test for last or whether my level of tolerance had finally been reached. Whatever the case, I could no longer just grin and bear it!

The physical and mental stress of the nine-day trauma inevitably reached its peak as it neared its end. The final test was a barium enema, aimed at evaluating my lower intestine. I soon came to realize that sometimes professionals can be *so* professional that they almost cease to be human. That was the impression I got from the technician administering this particular test.

Yet another insertion into my body—and I was still expected to simply just grin and bear it. "All right, turn over on your side, Ms. Majette," she requested in a completely rehearsed tone. Her voice seemed as cold as the steel table upon which I was lying.

Not aware at the time that I was experiencing chills and fever from the disease, I thought they were from her attitude. I entertained

20

myself by allowing my mind to guess how many times she had done this very same procedure on other patients, making them feel as if they were machines instead of people.

As she inserted the hard tube into my rectum, I was still expected to grin and bear it. *What is wrong with these people,* I screamed to myself. *What is wrong with her, giving me an enema so ritualistically with no mercy or compassion at all?* Had she ever considered how the patient might feel? "Did she even care?"

"Now hold it," she commanded.

Oh, God, please help me, I cried in my heart.

"Just a few more shots," she assured me, taking a few more pictures of my insides. It seemed as if time stood still, more so than I could as I tried not to squirm.

And what about my doctor? He was the real culprit. Dr. Carmine knew what pain and agony he had put me through with the other tests. How could he do this to me? I had begun to trust him. *He should have scheduled this test first,* I disputed bitterly within myself. *Maybe I've had just about enough!*

Finally I heard the familiar voice filter into my consciousness. I had tried so hard to remove myself from the situation. I guess I had somewhat succeeded because it was as if her voice had to travel through some kind of a time zone in order to reach me. "You can get up now," the technician stated in her same calm, emotionless voice.

I looked in amazement. "I can?"

The puzzled look on my face must have been familiar to her, for she quickly responded, "The bathroom is straight ahead."

She never explained what I was to do. I guess she knew it was self-explanatory, considering the discomfort I was experiencing from holding a foreign substance inside of my delicate innermost parts for so long.

I couldn't get to the toilet fast enough! Once there, I had no choice but to release the contents of my bowels, which I had been required to so painfully hold, but the physical release was by no means a solo event; I anxiously released myself and emptied the contents of my emotional bowels, too, which had also been placed on hold for weeks. The built up stress and strain of the entire ordeal had finally succeeded in overpowering my will to endure, and I simply crumbled. With my head resting on my forearm as it draped across the toilet tissue dispenser at my side, I cried for the first time since Dr. Carmine's office. No longer could I grin and bear it. Enough is enough for anyone! I just cried, and cried, and cried. What a relief—the sweet release of built up pressure. Through and through, my entire being was finally being released of all pressure: physical, mental, and emotional. Now I could go on!

No one told me of the consequences of these activities, that the tests would be stressful on my body, aggravating my situation and causing exacerbations of more disease activity. Hence, I left the hospital barely able to walk, little flexibility in my limbs, stiff and sometimes locking muscles, fatigued, weak, in excruciating pain, and weighing less than one hundred pounds at the age of twenty-three.

What a nice feeling to be home again in comfortable, familiar surroundings, I thought. But my lifestyle was in no way familiar. So many incapacitating disabilities, so many things were different. I knew some things would be different; I had a feeling I would have to make some adjustments, but this was a bit much. This was real extreme!

Showers came sporadically, and when they did, they became chores instead of relaxing pleasures. They usually left me with grave feelings of inadequacy, as I would have to summon my mother to wring the excess water from the washcloth before I could go back to bed for more hours of rest.

It seemed as if I was always thirsty and never had enough strength to hold a full glass of water. I would inevitably drop it, ten times out of ten.

Where had all my physical strength gone? How could it have just disappeared? I recalled how I used to play football with the boys in my neighborhood and climb trees as a kid. Where had *I* gone?

The intensity of the fatigue was so severe that I felt tired all day and all night, too weak to even get out of bed at all. *How could anyone be so tired after resting all day? Sluggish yes, but real fatigue? No, that's impossible*, I reasoned. I definitely did not understand.

Nevertheless, I soon learned that lupus fatigue is none like any other. It was as if I had been deprived of sleep for two or three weeks while constantly on the move at a super fast pace. And the weakness was exactly that—a complete loss of strength. The combination of weakness and fatigue made the everyday tasks of survival almost impossible. Many times they were impossible. Assistance from my mom, always my best friend, made my life bearable. She was not only a major source of strength for me, but also my sustenance for survival, determination, and will to fight another day. God moved through her and used her to give me a tangible hand in every way possible.

Whatever limitations were not the result of fatigue and weakness were undoubtedly precipitated by the painful and disabling arthritis. The doctor's office and drugstore were my only outings for months. The grocery store was a definite no-no. Walking at all was a challenge. The mere thought of pushing a cart or picking items from the shelves was inconceivable.

The weekly visits to Dr. Carmine's office soon changed to bi-weekly visits, and Mom carried my small clutch purse of essentials as I struggled to carry myself. Sometimes I would just sit and stare into space, daydreaming, looking closely at my new life, remembering the old, and allowing the sobering realities of my disabilities to finally sink deep into my mind.

Thinking back to that cold winter day in February, I had known nothing of these things that were to come as I left Bethesda Hospital with a newfound hope and what I thought to be a moderate understanding of this queer illness. Although, as time went on, I realized I didn't understand it at all, and the hope I had was nothing but false.

Before my departure that day, Dr. Carmine had come in and joined me on my bedside. I realized from his conversation that this was going to be a common practice with us. Side by side in treatment, side by side in failure, and side by side in success. I soon realized we had to have a real partnership in order to make this thing work.

So he sat down and began to inform me of a tiny little peach-colored pill that I could take each morning that was guaranteed to make me feel better and make the lupus more bearable. His explicit reiteration of *take each morning* should have signaled some type of alarm regarding this drug, but so much was happening all at once, I guess my senses where a little dull. I heard the doctor talking and actually experienced the entire series of events, all while feeling as if I were in some hypnotic state or an uncontrollable daze—being there and yet not really there at all. Was I freaking out, or was it just God's way of protecting me from the fire?

Dr. Carmine continued to brief me on taking this medication, telling me of its advantages. What he did not tell me was that little peach pill, appearing so innocent and so tiny in size, would add an additional fifty pounds to my normal body weight, change the molecular structure of my cells, cause uncontrollable mood swings, deplete my body of numerous vitamins and nutrients, make me more susceptible to infections, pneumonia, and possibly cataracts, glaucoma, and memory loss. This deadly chemical was *prednisone*, a synthetic form of cortisone, commonly known as steroids.

As time transpired, my body became steroid dependent. Only God could deliver me. I experienced everything from steroid-induced pneumonia to steroid-induced stretch marks, all in the name of medical treatment and scientific advancement. I was constantly being told, *if this had occurred twenty years ago, you would not be here now*, since steroids had not yet been invented. My attitude then and now is that it may have been better that way. This attitude is shared by most lupus victims I know, as well as by others in general who suffer from incurable diseases and who are surviving only by means of life-sustaining drugs. The medical profession is usually very consistent in choosing to ignore the age-old debatable question of *quantity of life versus quality of life* which plagues so many of our severely ill. Is it enough to just be alive if one is not able to lead a normal life?

Nevertheless, I returned home to my one-bedroom apartment in Cincinnati with a newfound false hope that was attributed to my ignorance of the drug and the disease. Dr. Carmine was obliging enough to give me some literature to read, along with a warning that quite a bit of inaccurate information had been published regarding the illness. In essence, the less I read the better.

He really was a nice, gentle man. Don't get me wrong. I feel Dr. Carmine did his job well. I don't hold him accountable for the negative repercussions of the drug usage. He followed his best judgement, and so did I at the time. It just so happens that I did not know what I know now. Such knowledge would have definitely influenced my decision. But we can only make decisions based on the knowledge we have at the time.

I ignored Dr. Carmine's advice regarding the literature, as a heightened level of curiosity soon dominated my behavior. I wasted very little time before persuading two friends to take me to the university library.

Bob and Eric, my next door neighbors, were students at the university at the time. We were all very young and had learned to lean on each other quite a bit that year after migrating to Cincinnati. The fact that we lived only a block or two from the university made the library easily accessible for the *ordinary* person; however, we still had to drive because I couldn't walk the distance.

Bob and Eric were a little leery of taking me anyplace in my condition. But being torn between not wanting to divulge their true sense of cowardice and yet wanting so desperately to do something, anything, to help make my cross a little easier to bear, they listened attentively to my argument. Putting my all into the role of confident capable Susan, I begged and pleaded my case.

Hidden beneath my facade was still the reality that even I myself didn't really know whether or not I could make the trip. Those days I never knew what task I could actually accomplish until I tried. Even my ability to use the toilet became a guessing game. Nevertheless, no one knew of my secret reality but me, so I went on with my persuasion. "I assure you I'll be all right," I cried. "Do you really think I would ask you to take me if I didn't think I could make the trip? Of course not," I lied.

Not even my mother knew how I *really* felt, and I usually told her everything. But not this time, for I knew of her fears and her love for me. She wanted no harm, self-imposed or otherwise, to come to her child. It was easy for me to put my entire heart into this act, for this was the first time in weeks that I had had any say-so over anything in my life, and we were still speaking of *my* life and a disease that threatened the very existence of it. I felt I owed it to myself to force myself to take this trip to the library since I had spent the past several weeks enduring pain and affliction at the beck and call of others. So on I went with my performance, taking my audience by storm. "You would want to know more about your illness too, if this had happened to you, wouldn't you?" I asked, knowing the answer would be *yes*.

Their eyes met in agreement with a look that admitted my victory.

"I would drive myself if I could," I stated. They knew I would have done so because it was that independent attribute in my personality that had gotten me to Cincinnati in the first place. "But I can make the trip to the building if you all will just get me to the campus." I sounded so convincing, trying desperately to overlook the fact that I would need assistance getting downstairs and into the car. Bob and Eric fell for my act, and reluctantly, they finally agreed to my scheme.

So off to the library we went, just so I could see for myself what this thing called lupus was really all about; and boy did I see. For a short while, I stood at the shelf just flipping through pages of different books, when suddenly my stomach began to churn and an uncomfortable queasiness crept up into my throat. The information and vivid photographs were so astonishingly grotesque that I was forced to close the books and walk out of the place in tears. No doubt I would have run if I could, but the immobility of my joints combined with the shock of what I was seeing prevented any other reaction. *Would I look like that*, I wondered, *bald headed with diseased-looking skin?* I sure would before it was all over.

As time passed, I realized that Dr. Carmine was absolutely right. There had been quite a bit of incorrect information printed on lupus, but fortunately the information I was introduced to on that night at the library was all correct; it did not fall in the erroneous category. What I had been exposed to was the cruel harsh reality of how deadly and hopeless this incurable disease could be. It was simply devastating!

I never returned to the library, at least not to research lupus. I later turned to other *safer* sources for information, such as the National Lupus Foundation and the National Institutes of Health, where the material had been sugar-coated for easier digestion. I've never been one to run from the truth, but this was one time I preferred to take the coward's way out. I later realized that it was just as well because the firsthand experience I later encountered taught me more than any book ever could.

Three long catastrophic months lingered by with my body slowly deteriorating as this rare and supposedly incurable disease frantically progressed. I became convinced that the nomenclature used to identify it could not have been more appropriate. Within a matter of days, I noticed the red rash on my face worsening; it extended across my cheeks and down my nose. Unbeknownst to me at the time, this unusual rash was not only a major characteristic of the disease, but also responsible for the labeling of the disease, *systemic lupus erythematosus*; the Latin word, *lupus*, means *wolf* in English, and the Greek term, *erythema*, translated in English means *to be red*—red wolf. How accurate; the rash did resemble that of a wolf's face, and it definitely was red in color. So I understood the Latin and Greek terms and the logic of the terminology, but exactly what did all of this mean to me now and what would it mean to me in the days to come? Precisely what would the future hold? It wasn't long before my adventure with the disease was well underway, and the answers to my many questions came trickling in with a phenomenal array of new experiences.

The first three weeks home after my release from the hospital were incredible. I say *release* with all sincerity. Being confined to a hospital is almost like being in prison. There are rules on top of rules; there are regulations—no independence, signing in, signing out, and believe it or not, patients are not allowed to visit other floors without the doctor's permission. I felt totally constrained.

Although the release to go home was greatly welcomed, the events of the following weeks were not. Although I took the magic drug as prescribed, my body did not respond to the treatment. I guess one would say my already worsened state progressed. Unfortunately, or maybe I should say fortunately, I wasn't cognizant of the fact. Everything after a point seemed the same to me. I had to deal, and I do mean deal, with the same pains: shooting pains, stabbing pains, numbing pains, day in and say out. Who cares whether the pain rates an eight or a ten; anything over a five was devastating to me.

I was oblivious to the fact that each day was worse than the day before. They all seemed the same to me: extreme pain, extreme fatigue, and extreme weakness. The one thing I knew—the only thing I knew—was that I was not getting any better, and the body that I was now living with and struggling with was not the same body I had known during the other twenty years of my life. It was not the body that had allowed me to go to college full-time, work evenings and weekends, and party three or four nights a week. It was not the same body that could survive on a few hours of sleep for days without failing. As the rash progressed and my hair fell out, it was not the same body that was responsible for the many dates I had enjoyed.

As I dutifully popped the little peach-colored pills each morning, the day's tasks became more and more difficult. The joints and limbs that were once in severe pain ceased to function at all, and the possibility of true disability became an ominous reality. Most of the time, my muscles were too weak to support my body. Even when lying flat on my back, I had to sleep with five pillows as props: two for my legs—my knee joints were too tender to touch the bed or each other, one for my head, and one for each arm. Before lupus, it was impossible for me to sleep on my back, but these days I didn't have the strength nor physical ability to turn myself over to any other position; it was that or nothing. If by chance someone else did succeed in turning me over, I wasn't able to maintain the position. Yes, most of the time my muscles were extremely weak, but to my utter surprise, one day they locked!

I wasn't quite sure whether it was the muscles or the joints that were the culprits of this handicap. The only thing I was positively certain of was that I no longer had use of my left leg. I could not lift it; I couldn't even move it! The horrible result of this was that I could not walk! My brain was sending the proper signals, but there was no response. Not knowing that this phase of disability would last only a short time, my initial response was sheer panic!

As time passed, the feeling in my leg slowly returned, first as pain, but still, it returned. Learning to walk again at the age of twenty-three was a strange experience. I can't remember taking my first steps as a child, but I'm quite sure it wasn't with as much intellectual application and precision as it was the second time around, for this time I had a new awareness and understanding of the law of gravity and equilibrium, all of which led to a more concentrated effort. I analyzed my every move, concentrated very carefully on each step, and today I don't walk slue-footed as I once did.

This was one of the first instances where I really experimented with the power of God's Spirit operating through me. Nothing could have given me the determination I needed to overcome the stumbling block of partial paralysis. No one else could have provided the courage I needed to learn to walk again. I prayed before, during, and after each attempt, each action, each step; I had to. I tried so desperately . . . and surprisingly succeeded in letting this new inner strength manifest itself to an outward reality.

My initial encounter with God's Spirit had just recently occurred a few days prior; one spring-like day in mid-March. Body too weak to maneuver practically any of its incapacitated parts anywhere, I lay on the bed motionless and definitely saddened in heart while listening to the first songbirds of the season.

I love springtime; I guess everyone does, but with me something comes alive even more on the inside. It's almost as if my inner being blossoms along with the flowers. I get an aesthetic rush from just looking, smelling, and touching God's creation as He initiates and ushers in life.

The weeks of disability had forced me to adjust to a different kind of life. A life of not doing and not going, with all of which I was less than thrilled. Not being able to go out in the spring air was disappointing, but not being able to enjoy the sights even from indoors was not as easy for me to accept. I heard the birds tweeting happily, singing their songs of joy and praise to their Creator. I could see the sun's rays beaming through the window, but I couldn't get my body to carry my eyes to that window. Can you imagine not being able to move?

As I lay silently on the bed, my thoughts wandered to scenes of people dancing, shopping, walking, and even running. I wondered why I couldn't do even the least of these things? What I wouldn't have given to be able to get up at that very moment, to have the physical strength and capability to sit on the side of that bed, to stand on my feet, to walk to the window, or even to wipe the tear that quietly rolled from the corner of my eye.

Surprising to me, as I laid there in my own deep despair, I soon felt a presence, a very calming presence. All of a sudden, I no longer heard the birds singing; I no longer felt the pain or the severe discomfort to which I had become accustomed. My mind was totally unconscious and insensitive to any aspect of my physical existence, or was it? I couldn't have been totally insensitive to it because I looked down at my afflicted and diseased body lying on the bed. I was on the ceiling looking down at *myself*! It was as if I had been suspended in space, lingering on the ceiling of my bedroom. The size five jeans, black top, and quilt-patterned blue vest in which my mom had dressed me simply stared back at me as if on some mannequin in a department store display. I knew my mind had to be alert because it had registered the very thing that my eyes were seeing. And I knew I was not imagining it. I had graduated from college with a minor in Psychology, so I was very much aware of the games the human mind can play; the escape mechanisms, the defense mechanisms—I knew it all, and I knew that was not what was happening here. But what *was* happening? What was actually going on with me as I watched myself lay motionless on the bed?

Before I could determine the answer, something else happened. Instantaneously, I began to experience some type of communication—no words, no sounds, and no actions as we know it, but very clear and definite communication. A very strange familiarity of harmonious interaction began to take place. My inner being, which I prefer to call my spirit, was attuned and in actual dialogue with another being, another spirit—one greater than myself, I could tell. One so great that His power disembodied and embraced me totally in an unusual sort of way, transporting me to a totally different, much higher plane. I found myself in a space in time where time was no more. I had definitely transcended this place, this world, this life.

Although there were no words exchanged and no sounds uttered, there was still a message, a very strong message. This awesome presence of power, of wisdom, of love, communicated to me that I didn't have to go through this. Referring to what I was experiencing with the illness and what lay ahead for me, I had a choice. This Spirit paused and waited for a reply.

I did not answer, but this Spirit must have sensed my yielding towards a *yes, I'll stay*, because He interrupted my silence with words of warning. "It will not be easy!"

Being the type of person that is easily enticed by a challenge, those words only ignited the flames of my fire to fight. The insatiable urge of curiosity was my motivating force, and I quickly replied, "But I will. I want to go on and see what the end will be."

Strangely enough, that seemed to be the right response. Maybe it wasn't my high level of curiosity at all; maybe it was the wisdom in my spirit uniting with the wisdom of my Creator to fulfill His plan. I knew deep down inside that this Divine Spirit force knew me, cared for me, knew the things of the future, and would, undoubtedly, be with me in the days to come as I went through my chosen fate. However, the most reassuring thing of all was the calm, peaceful, comforting feeling I experienced during the entire encounter.

As I said, it felt *right* saying I would stay. Maybe my friend knew all along that I wouldn't say *no*, that I would willingly go along with the plan—His plan. Maybe He just wanted to let me know that He was with me. Well, surely He was and still is today.

In no time at all, I was back in the reality of this earthly realm, and once again I heard the birds singing, not that they had ever departed, but I had.

2. Tried and True

During the initial days after the partial paralysis, I practiced walking around the house; sometimes improving, sometimes regressing. The only thing consistent about lupus was its inconsistencies! Each day Mom and I wondered if this would be the day to try walking outside. Would I be able to make it? No one knew the answer to that million dollar question, not Mom, not the doctor, not even me, but the uncertainties were not enough to keep me from trying. So one day the big day finally came, the day that I felt strong enough to try walking outside, a special day to enjoy touching and smelling God's creation once again. With great anticipation and the new found patience that was so quickly becoming a part of my old personality, Mom and I bundled ourselves up to brave the brisk breezes of the Midwest and started on our journey.

Once the limited use of my leg had returned just as mysteriously as it had once disappeared, Dr. Carmine and I instituted a walking program. Seeing that this would stimulate my body's organs, as well as repair damaged muscles, tendons, and ligaments, I set out on this new regime. There were no prescribed expectations nor preset limits. I was to use my instincts, listening to my body tell me what it should, could, and would do.

This came to be my first and long-lasting lesson in dealing with and surviving such an illusive illness.

Walking on flat terrain was challenge enough, so needless to say that getting down the steps of my apartment building was a true nightmare. Not only did my knees semi-cooperate by bending only partially , but they also lacked the necessary strength to support my body weight. Struggling with the task by shifting all of my weight onto the leg standing in order to raise the other leg onto the next step, I would then go to the next level of the stairs by pulling that same body weight of my upper torso using the side rails. I concentrated hard, trying desperately to transmit orders of obedience from my brain to my body. "Lord, please help me do this," I whispered with every step I struggled to make.

While struggling down the steps, it was obvious to me that Mom wanted to help. She looked at me with eyes that blazed with anticipation. Beaming with the desire to act on her love, she waited patiently for a clue or even an inkling from me as to how she could help. It seemed as if every fiber of her being screeched and screamed to take action, to help her baby, her one and only baby, in whatever way possible. Her entire being was aimed, ready to set into motion any gear necessary to assist me. She wanted so desperately to help; it was written all over her face, but she couldn't. There was absolutely nothing she could do.

I can only imagine the sense of frustration, helplessness, and pain *she* must have felt while watching me deal with *my* frustration, helplessness, and pain. It was impossible for me to tell her what to do to assist me in reaching my goal of the great outdoors. I wasn't even sure what I could do or what I needed to do to maneuver myself downstairs to get out of the door. We took it step by step, not knowing what to do nor what to expect next.

My mom was a small-framed woman; definitely not big enough to carry me, I thought. In addition to that, she had been waiting on me hand and foot, caring for my every need for weeks. I didn't want to add anything more to her shoulders; if anything, she needed a break, so I used the banister of the stairs and whatever parts of my body I could to refrain from leaning on her for physical support—except when absolutely necessary. I needed to handle it this way for psychological reasons, too; I needed to know I was doing everything I possibly could to help myself. My independent nature wouldn't allow anything less.

A small portion of my physical maneuvers were made possible by the huge B-12 shots I received from Dr. Carmine in alternate hips every other day. Sure, they were painful, but they helped.

The pain from the actual injection was not as bad as the pain I felt the day following the shot. Pain from the actual injection lasted only a very short while, and I learned to lessen it even more by following Dr. Carmine's advice of relieving pressure on the muscle while receiving the injections. After receiving them every other day for approximately four weeks, I even began to build up a tolerance to the pain. One can get used to anything after a while; practice truly does make perfect. My true consolation during this was that the shots really did help me walk.

As Mom and I went down the stairs of my building, I realized that, although my legs did not seem very strong, they were still much stronger than my upper torso. I could push my body weight up with my arms as long as I was standing and the banister was waist high, but my arm strength drastically decreased when summoned above my waist.

I pushed and pulled—still one step at a time—not only with my feet, but with every part of my body. I concentrated, I contemplated, and I carefully calculated my every move. *Oops, what happened?* my brain responded. *My left knee didn't bend like it did two steps back. What's wrong?*

Good old dependable, inconsistent lupus, I thought. *Didn't it get the message my brain was sending? Never mind, let's just try again.* Still no go! *Well, we can get around that,* I promised myself, determined to make it outside. *Let's double-time,* I told my good leg. *OK, that's good,* I responded with satisfaction. *Now what?* I thought as something else changed. My right leg gives away, and immediately I scream to myself, *Oh, no! Please don't fail me now! Boy, will I be glad when this phase is over.*

Are we gonna make it? I wondered to myself. Still not saying a word that would to alarm Mom. *Finally, the last step! What a relief! We'd made it!*

Reality and rationality immediately stood up in the left side of my brain. *If going down is this difficult, what will climbing up be like?* I quickly erased the thought and enjoyed my victory. We had made it! I had made it! We were almost to our destination of the great outdoors.

Naturally, the door was too heavy to open, and Mom was only too eager to help. I could see the pain all over her face as she attempted to refrain from reaching out to me while she had idly stood by watching me fight my battle alone. I knew she hurt every time I would hurt, although in a much different way, but that was the way it had to be, at least for now. This was a new experience for both of us, and I'm so glad we were there together.

Mom held the door open while I slowly walked through it into another world, the outside world, the real world. No longer in the safety net of home, but no longer caged in four walls, either. Once outside, the pain, discomfort, and effort of all my struggles simply seemed to vanish in the abundance of fresh air that surrounded me, as a new welcomed sense of freedom seemed to overwhelm me. I was as a bird in flight!

In no time at all, I felt as if my mind, body, and soul had just been released. It seemed as if I could breath easier and the colors were more vivid. Although my lethargic energy level and limited physical mobility had remained unchanged, the psychological boost I experienced overshadowed my negative realities like a blast from an atom bomb.

Although the season registered spring on the calendar, the temperature felt like winter against my southernly-acclimated skin. I just knew it was a beautiful spring day when I saw the bright sun beaming through the window, but once outside, the story quickly changed. The theory of shining sun equaling warm temperatures was valid in my hometown of Newport News, but not in the Ohio Valley. In Cincinnati, the weather rarely seemed pleasant; it was usually cold and snowing or hot and humid, rarely just a nice, calm warm day. I had been introduced to the absence of spring and fall, now only extremes. Umm, extremes! Did lupus and Cincinnati know each other? Were they friends, or had they only made a bet to see which could outdo the other?

The cold, refreshing, brisk wind sharply hit my face as I blinked my eyes rapidly in response to the change in temperature. Thank God some part of my body was still functioning properly.

I had been outside a few times since my release from the hospital, but only to go to the doctor; going for a walk was different. When going for a walk, I could choose the time of day in which I wanted to exert what little energies I could possibly muster up, and there were no preset limits or expectations. There was no goal line, no finish line, no pressure, and no stress. I didn't have to make it to the car; I could just stand at the door, if that's what I felt like doing. One might ask how walking to the car can present a stressful situation. Well, it did for me when I wasn't sure whether I could make it or not, knowing we would be late for our appointment if I took too long. Leaving earlier wasn't the answer; my energy level was so low, I would get washed out if I had to wait a long time. But this was different; what a relief!

Getting down the stairs had been a real chore, so after exiting through the door, I just stood there a while tasting the victory I had just won and enjoying the fresh air. Needing desperately to rest, I would have much rather sat a spell than stand, but my knees didn't even bend enough to squat, much less to sit on the curb or the stoop of the building. I used to laugh at those folding chairs attached to canes that were always advertised in the little magazines inside the Parade section of the Sunday newspaper; now, I only wish I had one. Isn't that ironic?

After a somewhat brief pause, I subconsciously reached for Mom's arm. She was right there, as usual. Our steps were short and small, and we didn't go very far at all. We only walked past the neighbor's house next door and back again. Nevertheless, the pleasure of being outside and actually walking was enough for me! Those days it didn't take a lot to make me happy; I was grateful for the least little positive thing that happened in my life.

I had been working as a professional sales representative in the private sector of the corporate industry prior to the illness, but hadn't been able to work in months. The company had wonderful benefits, so my exuberant hospital bills were being paid, as were the prescriptions and my living expenses.

I learned quite a few lessons from not being able to work. I learned that God always makes a way, regardless of the circumstances.

I also learned that society places quite a bit, probably too much, emphasis on the importance of the workplace. So many times, our entire self-worth is determined by our workplace or the position we hold. Did we exist before we began to engage in gainful employment? If the job is terminated, will we be, also? Some people feel they will; some people feel that their job is their total existence. I beg to differ. It is a good thing to be constructive and productive in this world, but formal work is not the only way to do that. Many people are productive each and every day, even without engaging in gainful employment.

Another lesson I learned is that societal values usually serve no real purpose or assistance in dealing with life-threatening situations that may arise. I found this to be true through personal experience. Neither my so-called professional job, nor the many awards or degrees I had received from prestigious institutions of higher learning had anything to offer to help with this curveball life had surprisingly thrown me.

I also realized that most professionals were not concerned with me as a person at all. They said they were. They circulated little bulletins about employee worth to the company; they instituted programs, profit sharing, and the like to help employees feel like a part of the organization, but all with only one focus in mind: *how to promote a greater level of productivity for their company.* They only seemed to be concerned with what I had to offer. When what I had to offer and what I could do for them changed, then so did their time and attitude towards me. Sad, isn't it?

When out of work for a short period for whatever reason— maybe we are ill, maybe our child is sick, or maybe we need to take care of personal business, whatever the case—we usually will be preoccupied with the job, thinking what will be there when we return or what we left undone. Nine times out of ten we are constantly thinking about the job, but is the job really thinking about us? Probably not. The job is usually thinking about the job, also; the main and sometimes only concern is when we will return to resume our duties. Never mind the pressing issues that have kept us away; the only question is *when will you be back.* Never mind our feelings as a human being or what we may be going through as people; the issue is still *the job*. They may call to see how we are doing, but their ultimate purpose is to find out when we will be back.

When passing, people often exchange greetings by saying, "Hi, how are you?" Do they really care? The next time you're asked that question, I admonish you, don't reply, and see if anyone notices.

In the work world everyone usually adopts the same values, the same way of thinking, cloned by mental conditioning, brainwashed by a type of sub-societal orientation. Well, I could no longer be a part of that society. My physical limitations and present situation made all the things that had been so very important to me all my life—education, success, achievement—seem so totally irrelevant, nothing but a big balloon full of air and absolutely trivial from where I now stood.

All the things I had been striving for and living for in life all of a sudden had no place in the ever-present struggle in which I now found myself. The physical world had limits, and most of *my* physical world had crumbled. I was now in another world, and I needed another reality that would fit into my new world—a new reality that could assist me in being successful in this new world that I had entered into, was now experiencing, but yet did not understand. It was different, very different from anything I had every known. One thing I did understand, though, was that this new world was on a different plane than any I had ever been exposed to. I wasn't sure what the plane was, nor where it was. The only thing I knew for sure was that I needed more knowledge and wisdom to deal with it effectively. Realizing I couldn't get what I needed from the society of which I had just recently been such an active member and was now banished, I knew I had to search elsewhere.

As more questions arose, I searched harder for the answers. I searched for that peace I had felt during the conservation with my Creator back in March. I searched for the strength I had seen manifest itself in the past few weeks. I searched for the answer—the answer to the method to the madness that I was experiencing. I searched for the courage to overcome, wisdom to understand, and the strength to deal. My physical world had crumbled, and although

I had graduated magna cum laude and been accepted by *Who's Who among Students in American Universities and Colleges,* my knowledge and mental capabilities were still very limited. I had to make contact with something or someone who had the answers I needed. Although I didn't know the answers, I did know the questions, and I knew they were not physical-related; they dealt with intangible issues like courage, strength, wisdom, knowledge. Intangible soon led to *inside,* and I came to the shocking realization, the true awareness that *everything* I needed was on the inside of me—the essence of me, the part of me that was powerful enough and flexible enough to transcend this place, this existence and go beyond what I grew up thinking was reality. This I found to be my spirit.

As time progressed, so did the deterioration of my physical body. The beautiful, long, semi-curly hair that had been so graciously bestowed upon me by a combination of Indian, African, and Anglo-Saxon descent had begun to fall out in large patches. Although there was an excessive amount of hair in the comb and bathroom sink when I attempted to style it, the real shock came when I would find the pillowcase covered with loose strands each morning. Some places had become bald, completely clean, and the few strands left had changed texture from easily manageable curls to a thin, straggly, straight mess. As if that wasn't enough, my scalp was red and scaly, just like my face and hands. It would peel as I tried to relieve the itching. Those days my physical appearance had changed so drastically, if I did not know it was me on the inside, I would have not even recognized myself in the mirror. I was there through the entire escapade and had witnessed the gradual changes take place, but those who knew me and saw me months later did not recognize me at all. It was rather amusing when I returned to my hometown after being sick for a number of years. I would pass people on the street, those with whom I had grown up and gone to school, and they would look me straight in the face, cordially speak, and never realize it was me. Sometimes I would tell them, and sometimes I wouldn't. Sometimes I just didn't feel up to going through the explanations. *Who was this new monster,* I would sometimes ask myself.

As my hair diminished, the skin rash made rapid strides. My entire face, hands, and arms, were beet red with inflammation. The golden-brown hue I had grown to love and appreciate was a thing of the past. My ears were no exception; they were just as red and itchy. As I rubbed them they began to swell twice their normal size and peel also. I jokingly called them *elephant ears*; that's what they looked like to me. During those days I had also begun to develop the typical *moon face*—another side effect of the steroids that I feel is too readily accepted by the medical profession—round, fat cheeks on what had always been attractive, slender face. The fluid from the steroids also tended to settle in the abdominal area, so I looked as if I were about five months pregnant still wearing size five clothes. I guess I looked like a freak of some sort, but I was too involved with surviving to really worry about it. I had neither the time nor strength to deal with appearances; it just didn't seem to be a priority at the time. I was consciously aware of it, but I was much more preoccupied with simply surviving. I was much too busy concentrating on being able to bathe myself and use the toilet. Before getting sick, I never gave thought to sitting on the toilet; it was a natural act, but now I could barely bend my knees to squat. Things had really changed.

Sometimes I would have to stay in bed until five or six o'clock in the evening before I would have enough energy or strength to even take a bath. Sometimes I would start the procedure, wash my face, brush my teeth, and have to lay back down. Sometimes an hour would do the trick and sometimes not; sometimes I would have to wait until the next day. The experience was the same with eating a meal. I would be famished—another side-effect of the steroids. Mom would cook, then help me out of bed to the table. Most times, the fatigue would overtake me before I could finish what was on my plate. It would feel as if my neck muscles were too weak to support my head, then the stabbing chest pains would start. If the nausea didn't run me from the table first, the diarrhea usually did. Eating in bed was not the answer; my digestive system functioned much too poorly. In spite of it all, meal time was still an exciting time for me; it was a change from the eighteen hours of bed rest. Nevertheless, if I was fortunate enough to make it through a meal, I would inevitably be wiped out for hours afterwards. It was weird. And of course, all of these inconveniences necessitated the prerequisite *sometimes* because of lupus' sporadic, unpredictable, irrational nature. No two days were ever the same. Usually, various portions of the day were different; mornings were nothing like evenings, and evenings were nothing like afternoons. Sometimes the physical symptoms would change course in the midst of a given hour. Living and dealing minute by minute was the name of the game. I wouldn't even know if I could successfully turn over in the bed until I tried, and just because I was able to do it on a given day at 10:00 A.M., that did not mean I would be able to do the same thing the next day, nor that same day at another time. My entire existence was like a full-time circus.

On days that I could, I would move around the house. I didn't make it on too many walks outside until later that year. By the time spring had fully sprung, late May, I was able to engage in the walking program instituted by Dr. Carmine full-time, at least on most days. During this time a typical day would begin with breakfast. I was getting stronger, so I could get through an entire meal. I still couldn't hold a full glass of water, but I could sit. I usually had a surge of energy after eating, so I would attempt to go for my walk then. Before a meal, I was totally wiped out, but after a meal I was like a different person. I would screw tops on condiments after a meal and not be able to open them the next morning.

Then one morning, while sitting at the kitchen table in a comfortable leather chair, I waited patiently for Mom to complete her domestic chore of preparing breakfast. She seemed so content, as if in her own little natural habitat, and that she was. Domestic work was so familiar to her, for it had been such a large part of her life for so long. It had been her livelihood for as long as I could remember. She always appeared to be in seventh heaven whenever she was helping someone else; that's just the way she was, and today was no exception. My mind was beckoned back by the persistently loud blast of the tea kettle whistle, and I subconsciously reached for the jar of jam sitting on the table in front of me. Never giving up and never admitting defeat, I continued to try different tasks, always mindful of the sporadic and unpredictable nature of the illness. I constantly reminded myself that uncertainty was the only certainty and, subsequently, reached for the jar without thinking.

Picking it up slowly, I was excited that I didn't drop it. Much to my surprise, the arthritis was not overwhelming, and my fingers were flexible enough to surround the top of the jar. Then on to the next step, the grip. *Wow!* The strength was actually there. Before I could register what was really taking place, I had succeeded in actually opening the jar of jam. What a joy! "Ma! Look," I screamed. She immediately turned away from the stove. Allowing time for her brain to register what her eyes were seeing, she smiled. We both looked at each other in amazement, noting the open jar of jelly in one of my hands and the cap in the other. What joy, what excitement, what a true sense of accomplishment. "Look!" I screamed a second time. She smiled that same proud, reassuring smile that I had seen so many times before, when I would make her mud pies as a child or had brought in weeds, mistakenly thinking they were flowers, or even when I got good grades on my report card. Her smiles always seem to connect with the earnest determination in my spirit in support of my every effort, regardless of the tasks or accomplishments involved. I always felt nothing but true love simply for me being the person that I was. She immediately freed her hands and ran to the table. We embraced each other as we shared in the joy of the first real positive change in months.

As the days progressed, I got stronger and stronger, so one day I decided to try my independence and go walking outside alone. Mom was very agreeable; if there was any fear in her heart, which I'm sure there was, she didn't let it show. She was always my biggest fan and cheerleader. I'm quite sure she felt like a mother bird dropping her offspring in the air to see if it could fly. And boy did I fly!

My legs were strange during this period of the illness. They were no longer weak, but instead, they were extremely stiff. For months they felt as if they had steel rods in them. I later discovered that my connective tissues of bones, tendons, ligaments, and muscles were not flexible because my body was not manufacturing the normal and necessary lubricating fluids. The tightness had subsequently developed into a type of stiffness. It wasn't all bad, though; at least they were strong enough to support me now, and I could walk. Pain and discomfort is not such a big deal, once you realize it is a blessing to even have enough feeling in a limb for it to be able to ache. I eagerly, yet very cautiously, walked down the steps onto the sidewalk.

The difficulty of the task was still very real, but I had somewhat adjusted to my present situation. In some ways I had learned to overcome my disabilities; in other ways I had learned to flow with them. Whatever the case, I was no longer overly concerned with getting down the stairs this time. Instead, I focused my attention on taking the walk outside alone. That's what was really important; the day had finally arrived for me to go it alone, stand on my own two feet, in more ways than one. I was elated at my rekindled sense of independence and my new found freedom.

The clouds created a slight overcast which seemed to be normal for Cincinnati. Overcast skies are really strange, I think— cloudy, yet attempting to be sunny, almost as if God isn't quite sure what He wants to do, but that's not it all. The uncertainty lies within us. The truth of the matter is that we just don't know what God is going to do, if He's going to bring rain or sunshine, and that can be disturbing to us. Most of us like to know what's going on, and we usually like to be in control of situations; overcast skies strike out on both counts. Maybe that's what I should call lupus, *overcast skies*. Thank God the sun still shines behind the clouds.

I turned right, walking slowly, and filled with pride that I was doing so. Down the sidewalk I went towards the university. It was mid-afternoon on a weekday, and Ohio Avenue seemed a little deserted. School or work dominated the lives of most people and had taken them away from their homes, but my preoccupation with life was somewhat different. My goal was a lot more simple, but just as challenging for me. I was trying to go for a walk. I soon noticed a wonderful thing happening: the more I walked, the better I felt. I couldn't really explain it; it was so surprising. I had been walking before but had never felt this good. *Could this mean I was finally getting better?* I wondered. I kept on trodding until I began to feel tired. I had been walking for a while it seemed, but in looking back, I realized I had only gone midway down the block. *Maybe it's time for a break*, I thought.

I leaned against a stone wall in front of a stranger's house and thought about what I wouldn't give for seat right about then, but the only thing that would come even close to a seat at that point was the curb of the sidewalk. If bending to use the toilet was a problem, like sitting in a chair was a problem, then sitting on the curb was absolutely out of the question. The longer I stood there resting, the weaker I felt myself getting. I had been so excited over how good I was feeling that I lost all track of reality. I had failed to realize that I had to get back home.

My first inclination was to panic, but instead, I attempted to approach my problem from a rational, intellectual standpoint. *Let's see; what are my options*, I asked myself. I could stay there until my Mom became worried and came looking for me, or I could try to make it back home on my own. I couldn't call for help; there was no one in sight. I wasn't in a business district since I hadn't made it to the university yet, so there was no public phone to use, not that I had any change on me. As I looked over my shoulder, it appeared that no one was home at the house owning the stone wall upon which I leaned to gather my strength and thoughts.

Feeling helpless and somewhat distressed at my situation I found myself in, I looked up at the sky into the bright sunlight which was hidden behind the overcast clouds just moments ago. I had gone to church as a child and had been told that there was a God who had created everything in the heavens and in the earth. I had been told that He answers prayers and helps people down here on earth, that, although He was high in the heavens, He still oversees His creation down here and makes sure the show is run right. I didn't know if I really believed all of this or not, but I did know I needed help and there was no one around. I looked up at the sky where I thought this *person* might be and whispered what some would call a prayer. I verbalized my doubt about His existence and simply said, "If you are up there and can see me and hear me like they say you can, then please help me get back home," as if He should prove something to me, but surprisingly enough, He did!

I was immediately compelled to stand up off the wall and walk towards my home. There was a strangeness about my being; I felt no worse, no better, no weaker, yet no stronger. Before I could fully comprehend what was happening, I was home! I was actually there. The last thing I remembered was leaning on the wall, talking to this invisible force, and the next thing I knew I was approaching the steps to my apartment. During the travel back to my house, I could feel myself walking, but I was not exerting any energy at all; it was almost as if I was on some type of conveyor belt being carried along the way down the sidewalk. It was absolutely incredible.

Needless to say, I was convinced that this God I had just prayed to, who so many people told me about, was alive and well. The reality of His existence shined bright within my soul. I didn't quite understand what had happened, but I knew it had happened and that it was good. And I knew that this invisible force who had created our universe was real.

3. Roller Coaster Ride

My physical appearance continued to change so drastically that each day I looked more and more like a different person. The rash had progressed to the point that I not only looked like I had an incurable disease, but I looked as if I *was* the disease. Big, thick, red splotches were all over my face, arms, and hands, thinning hair, and even more splotches on my scalp; what a sight! Still, by some strange coincidence, I did not seem to have a psychological complex about it. I didn't seem to be overly concerned with the fact that I looked abnormal, like something out of the *Guiness Book of World Records*. Maybe it was because I was no longer functioning in the main stream of society. The only time I came into contact with the public was at the doctor's office or the drugstore. I was accustomed to people staring, and even that didn't usually bother me, except for one particular instance I can recall.

Lupus had been on a rampage destroying my body for months by the time I regained enough strength to accompany Mom to the drugstore to pick up my prescriptions. One day while with her at Walling's Mini-Mart, a very memorable event took place.

While waiting patiently in the after-work crowd, I happened to notice a woman staring very intently at my diseased body. She seemed to be intrigued by my bald head, discolored splotches, and disproportionately shaped body.

She looked very appealing in her wool blend camel suit with matching blouse and navy pumps. The briefcase in her hand seemed to be just as big a part of her as the blond hair that so contently rested on her shoulders. Her striking professional image lashed out at me, grabbing all of my attention, as she reminded me of where I was once headed and what I was possibly missing.

Still, she persisted to stare with an uncontrollable gaze, as if in some kind of a trance. I was accustomed to people staring at me whenever I went out, but this was a bit unusual. Most people looked at me with wonderment and sometimes even pity, but she, instead, looked at me with sheer contempt. The expression on her face seemed to say, "What are *you* doing here? Who let you out?" As I stared back at her, I began to wonder what exactly was going through her mind. Maybe I intimidated her. Maybe I frightened her. Maybe I reminded her of what could be. Maybe I reminded her that her plastic world was all one big phony and that there was a real side to this thing called life that even she could not control.

Still her eyes stayed fixed on me, as if to make me go away. *Who does she think she is*, I thought. Was it OK for her to be there because she was beautiful, healthy, and well, and not OK for me because I was not? Was I suppose to drop my head in shame or hide because life had dealt me a bad hand or because the storms in my life had battered my vessel and my hope? Oh, no; I think not. I stared right back at her. Who did she think she was, looking down on me? She may have seen how tattered and torn my physical shell was, but she had no idea how much dignity, self-respect, and self-worth was harbored within. Neither was she aware of the awesomely powerful force inside of me that was growing more and more each day. I quickly rolled all of these positives into one big chunk of pride and gazed right back at her more intently than ever, only to win at her childish little game. *What kind of society do we live in that would make people grow up to be like this*, I wondered.

Soon, I witnessed a new expression dawning on the face of this fine example of the American dream. She finally looked embarrassed, turned, and walked away.

There had been so many changes I had now been forced to accept. The stylish, meticulous way in which I used to dress, as well as the glamorous make-up, was now a thing of the past. While working in the field of retail merchandising and going to one of the most prestigious colleges in the country, I had adopted a special style portraying a classy, sophisticated persona that seemed to disband right before my eyes. I had begun to develop the moon face and the retention of body fluid at the rate of approximately five pounds a week. My fashionable clothes did not fit anymore, and make-up made me look worse instead of better. All of the Flora Roberts and Fashion Fair in the world would not have changed my appearance one iota. Even if it had, the energy required to put it on had now disappeared. However, the real bottom line was the true change of heart and mind I had experienced. My preoccupation with the ordinary survival tasks of the day and the necessary functions of using the toilet or taking a bath consumed my every thought and entire existence; appearance was no longer a priority in my life.

My friends and family were very supportive during this time in my life. Stranded in Ohio with most of my friends and relatives on the East Coast, I would have felt as if I were all alone had they not kept in constant contact. Long distance calls of support and thoughtful cards of encouragement poured in, adding extra strength to my fight. Although no one could really understand what was taking place without actually being there to witness it firsthand, their love still continued to flow.

For a while it seemed as if everything was at a standstill. I wasn't getting any better, but I wasn't getting any worse either; I couldn't get much worse, in my opinion. The chest pains hindered my breathing; an inflamed digestive system hindered my meals; the steroids hindered my vision; the disease hindered normal brain function; and my body was almost useless. The only thing that really kept me going was faith—the faith my mother had in me, the faith I had in me, and the faith we both had in the miraculous power that had carried me back to the house that cool spring day—our God.

Daily I kept a journal, to the best of my limited abilities, to constantly remind myself that things had to get better. I also needed to reaffirm my sanity that I sometimes seemed to be losing.

Today has been a real trip with many mixed emotions. I got really burned out this morning while trying to help with breakfast. Breakfast was around 8:00 A.M.and I had to go back to bed before I collapsed, and stay 'til noon before I could muster enough strength to stand on my feet again.

I was blessed by the delivery of some new furniture. I was a little excited, my first set of furniture and all. It's not that I'm not appreciative, I AM. But good health is what I *really* want—*my* good health back.

Sometimes I feel as if I'm getting better and other times I just don't know. But one thing I do know for sure—the joy I'll feel and enjoy when the day arrives that I can run and play again. Tomorrow will be even brighter. Faith must prevail.

March 25, 1980

The visit to the doctor today was very positive and I finally feel like I'm getting the hang of climbing this steep hill in my life. The shot left me a little sore as expected, but physically I feel so much better.

March 26, 1980

What a day, I finally feel confident in kicking this illness. However, I guess I'll always have a stray of doubt since my life and destiny is not totally in my hands, but in the hands of a higher Supreme Being—God Almighty. I've come to really be aware of the fact and understand that everything can be taken away in the blink of an eye. One thing I do know is that if self-determination is what it's gonna take for me to be well again—then that I will be—well again!

My mental attitude is more of a trip sometimes than my physical state. I have to do some serious thinking and soul-searching to find out exactly where my head is. There are so many changes that have occurred since the illness that I almost feel like a different person. I sincerely think I'll be one by the time this is all over.

April 9, 1980

Not too good of a day at all. I was blessed to go to the supermarket with Mom this afternoon. Sitting in the car waiting for her to do the grocery shopping was definitely a challenge. I've never been one with a lot of patience, and sitting in the car, WAITING, sparked a new wave of melancholy. The minutes seemed to quickly turn into hours; of course, it was all my imagination. I sat watching ladies with little kids park, go in, and come back out; constantly watching the door for my mom to emerge. Not possessing enough energy to accompany her inside, just sitting in the car seemed to take it's toll on my body.

As evening has approached, I now feel worse; the chills, the fever, the nausea, and a serious case of the blahs. I'm still learning how to deal with this disease and days like today with the general flu-like feeling coupled with mood-swings easily throw me for a loop. Can you imagine living with the flu for weeks or months on end? Yea, you've got it—it's a real trip! Still I thank God for another day. Blah!

April 11, 1980

Today was not ordinary at all. In fact it was rather unusual. I started breaking out again with the rash on my head and hands. The doctor told me to increase my intake dosage of prednisone to 15 mg./day. I sincerely hope I'm not getting worse. This is the first time the rash has returned since I was released from the hospital. I thought that phase was over, but then whose paying me to thing, right? I do want to get well. I don't want to die. May God have mercy first on my soul, but also on my body. If I'm being punished, may God forgive me.
Sincerely Susan
"Me"
P.S. I still have faith though and tomorrow will be better. (smile)

April 12, 1980

I seem to be on the upswing again. But only God knows for sure. Thank God it stopped raining this afternoon, the walk did me a lot of good. I only hope that it's all down-hill now, no more setbacks.

Love, "Me"

April 14, 1980

I thought I was struggling to reach the top of the hill and was about $3/4$ the way up, but now I feel like I'm still at the bottom. I thought I was progressing to the point where the disease would soon be in remission, then today the doctor told me that direct exposure to the sunlight regressed some of our progress. That explained the new skin lesions; ANOTHER STUMBLING BLOCK. I got another shot and the side effects will probably start tomorrow.

April 15,1980

Well, I was right, the side effects did start today. I can barely lift the leg I got the shot in, the ache extends from my hip to my ankle. My knees are swollen even worse and the fluid causes this weird quivering sensation, it feels as if they are going to come out of the joint socket. The doctor couldn't give me an explanation. I guess I'll just have to live with it. However, the doctor did say it would probably subside once the treatment is complete. But when will that be? I guess I have no choice but to deal with it and wait on time—what a choice. I do know I'm tired of sleeping with pillows under my knees. But of course, another blessing just came to mind. I remember when I couldn't even bend them enough to lie on my side and sleep, now that was a real bummer, having to learn to sleep flat on my back; so things are improving in some ways.

Jackie called today. It's another blessing to know I have friends that care—true friends on whom I can depend. I find myself looking at all sorts of things as blessings these days. Nothing like a bad storm to put things into proper perspective. Thank God for today . . . And for the sunshine!

Regardless of the doctor's report, I still thanked God for the sunshine. Although the doctors lay claim to the fact that lupus made my body ultra-sensitive to the sun and that the sun would only cause me hurt, I believed that the sun was created to nourish and give life to every living thing on earth, and that included me!

April 18, 1980

What can I say about today, such a beautiful spring Friday. I woke up with a little stiffness but by tonight, it was absolutely unbelievable. The stiffness I had experienced right after the hospitalization returned in full force after four weeks of little or no existence. I don't understand why! What's even more strange is the fact that my right leg which gave me all the trouble at the onset of this crazy illness is not too bad now, but the left one which was fine is now the real problem. I don't understand that either, but then neither does the doctor. All he keep saying is, "Continue taking your medicine, I'll see you on Tuesday." I guess man is not suppose to understand everything. However, it would be a lot easier to deal with if I could understand how the body I used to call mine could be such a stranger and act so incredibly weird.

My heart has been palpitating all evening, but even that's better than those dagger-type sharp chest pains that sent me to the emergency room in January.

I was blessed today to buy some big straw hats to shield me from the sun. Thank God. Tomorrow will be better.

Love, Susan

I wasn't quite sure how I felt about the sun; I wavered back and forth—sometimes believing the doctors claim that it would harm me and sometimes yielding to the belief that it would help me. I just wasn't quite sure. There wasn't much I was sure of those days.

April 19, 1980

What a beautiful day—73 degrees and sunshine all over the place. I still cherish the miracle of a beautiful spring day; although I can't enjoy the sunlight with as much pleasure as I used to. Today I wore one of my new hats and plan to wear the other new one to church on tomorrow. Isn't this something, I'm actually excited about a new hat!

My life has changed so, I can barely dress myself or walk, so dressing up to look pretty isn't such an easy task anymore. Shopping is a definite no-no and physical beauty has ceased to exist with the thinning/falling hair, red rash, and side effects of the medicine. Anyway, I still thought the beauty of the day was fantastic even though I was a little afraid to feel the warmth of the rays upon my face. It's Saturday and Bob and Eric had a big cookout next door. Bob carried me piggy-back style up the stairs to the deck of their loft so I could attend. The situation held the potential of a real good time, but it didn't turn out that way. This evening I feel so-o-o bad. It seems I can't do much anymore without feeling terrible. I only stayed a little over a half-an-hour and now I am exhausted. My back hurts, my legs are ultra-stiff, my heart has been racing, and now arthritis has struck my left shoulder like a bolt of lightning. I've had all these symptoms before but I thought they had gone—again! Well, who am I to predict what will be? Maybe tomorrow will be better. Thank God for today.

Love, Susan

The experiences of those days taught me two very important lessons. The first lesson was how to live my daily existence spontaneously. Society teaches us to be structured individuals, to plan and operate very systematically. Attempting to implement structure with lupus would have been deadly! The grave unpredictability of the illness and it's symptoms forced me to be flexible and easy going, in thought as well as in action. I couldn't afford to get bent out of shape every time one of the symptoms changed course; I needed my energies to survive and to deal with everything that was

54

going on. I had no time for childish, negative behavior like an attitude; that would have only facilitated an already bad situation.
Sometimes I had to maneuver myself many different ways in order
to just accomplish one task; I had to be flexible, yielding, and
adaptable. I soon learned to go with the flow instead of bucking
heads with my reality. It paid off in the long run.

The second lesson I learned was, of course, patience. The
answer to every question regarding my situation appeared to be *I
don't know; we'll just have to wait and see.* This answer could foster
nothing but patience or frustration. I soon discovered that frustration served no real benefit to me. It did not help me deal with my
given situation at all; however, on the other hand, patience did.
There were times when the virtue of patience was the only thing
that helped me keep my sanity. It was also the only thing that fos-
tered enough peace to enable me to deal effectively with the wait
and weight of this all encompassing situation in my life.

April 20, 1980

Another beautiful spring day and I feel like the pits. My
knees have been exceptionally stiff all day and now the stiffness
has moved up and down the limb to encase my entire leg. I walk
like I'm about 90 years old. Even a crippled elderly woman at
church passed me coming down the stairs today. But thank God
the rash is better. Like I said, I feel worse physically, but I've
decided that I've come too far to give up now.

This morning my lymph glads were swollen, so I doubled the
antibiotics. The whole scenario gets crazier as the days go on.
The glands are swollen because of lupus, they think they are
fighting some kind of infection, but the infection is really me!
My body thinks of itself as the germ and is manufacturing an
overabundance of antibodies to actually fight itself, while still
thinking that it's fighting a 'real' foreign body. This fight going
on causes inflammation which is portrayed through other symptoms like the arthritis. The steroids, my daily peach friend, is
suppose to reduce the inflammation, calming the symptoms; but
unfortunately it simultaneously reduces my body's own natural

defense to 'real' germs and makes me more susceptible to 'real' infections. The antibiotics are to fight these 'other' infections; the 'real' ones, not the phony ones my body thinks it has. The problem is no one knows if the swollen glands are reacting to real germs or make-believe germs. (Don't worry—it doesn't make sense to me either) The steroids and the disease are both suppressing my immune system, thus my ability to fight infections, which makes my body think it has an infection after all, that's what the doctor thinks too and that's why he has me taking the antibiotics. The doctor pragmatically explains that this is the 'only a minor side effect' of the drug; that the advantages far outweigh the negative side effects because it is actually controlling the activity of the disease, SO WHY AM I STILL SICK?—Talk about Catch-22! So if the answer to this side effect is the antibiotic, I dare not ask why take antibiotics to fight germs when my body is already making too many antibodies to start with, that's the reason I have this problem called lupus anyway. I'll just assume that my antibodies are fighting the wrong thing, and the synthetic antibiotics are going to take up the slack. Like I said, it gets crazier and crazier!!!

I forced myself to take my walk and to stay up afterwards instead of going to bed.

I've endured too much to lie down and die so I must fight. If this thing gets me down, it will have won a real battle because I will put up a fight!

April 22, 1980

Another visit to the doctor highlighted this day. I felt very discouraged at the onset of the visit. Primarily because certain old symptoms started flaring up again; the joint pain, the bone pain, muscle and tendon tightness and pulling—all the pits. My skin is clearing up though which helps me believe I may be improving. The doctors say it will just take some 'time'. So I'll just pray for more patience.

Mom surprised me with another straw hat today and now I'm ready to continue the climb up my steep hill in grave faith and hope that one day, even if not very soon, I'll win the victory with flying colors. I don't know what I would do without Mom here for support and everything else. It's almost like I'm an infant again. I don't remember my first bout with infancy, but I will forever remember this one. She'll have two to remember!

April 23,1980

What a trip day. This morning was very, very nice, really exceptional and quite unbelievable. The stiffness was nonexistent. I could bend my right leg a little. My shoulder wasn't hurting either and I was blessed to take a pretty lengthy walk. However, by 12 noon it was a different story. All the symptoms returned and I spent most of the evening resting. Last night it took me three hours to fall asleep; the nerves all over my entire body kept twitching, so this evening I took a short nap before dinner.

Now as the day ends, I feel better but not as surprised, every hour is different. There is no rhyme nor reason to this terrible disease. It completely defies logic, so it seems only fitting that I would feel better after losing three hours of sleep than I would after taking a nap. (smile)

Nevertheless, all and all, I still had a pretty nice day.

One may ask, how could a day like this be pretty nice? My only reply would be: *all things are relative!*

April 25, 1980

Today was a pretty ordinary day. I felt a little better than usual this morning and Mom wanted to sleep late, so I decided to cook breakfast. I got 'burned out' about midway through the preparation and she had to come in and take over. I was forced to succumb to weakness and ended up in bed 'til 3:00 P.M. (breakfast had begun at 8:00 A.M.) What a bummer! Tonight I'm a little stronger, but the stiffness is here in full force. Nevertheless, I'm still hanging in there and fighting hard. Tomorrow will be a new and better day.

April 26, 1980

A pretty slow day. I was still somewhat 'washed out' from yesterday, so my walks were very short. I sometimes wonder if I'll ever get well and be my old self again?

April 27, 1980

Today was a little different. The stiffness was 'at ease' until after dinner. Today was the first day in a while that I really felt improved. Thank God for today.
Love, "Me"

April 28, 1980

A.M.—What a beautiful day, starting off. The stiffness isn't as noticeable and I'm strong enough to sit up and not feel weak. And all of this before breakfast—wonders never cease! It's cloudy and cool outside. It looks as if it's gonna pour down rain any minute, and I'm a long ways from being well; but it's still a beautiful morning. I can at least write in this book, hold this pen, think somewhat clearly and successfully jot it down.

P.M.—This afternoon was a little different though. Lupus didn't act up too much, but it sure did let me know it was still around. I was stiff and a little weak; that's always a bummer, but the real trip was in my mind, my attitude. I'm tired of being sick and I hate Cincinnati; but I can't leave, not even on a vacation. All I can do is stay here and be sick, until my change comes.

I did, however, receive a nice care package from my aunts and cousin back home today; almost like Christmas in April—it was nice and the only thing that brightened my day. But that's alright because tomorrow is another day and with God's help, it'll be better. I hope the doctor does decide to give me a letter recommending transfer back to the East Coast soon. This place is the pits!

Well what do you know, another month has passed and I'm still sick. The fluid retention is really beginning to bother me now. I can't bend my knees at all on my own and feel like I weigh 200 pounds. Dr. Carmine says, "Take 2 aspirin 4 times a day." What good that's gonna do, I don't know. I really hate taking aspirin. I get the feeling they don't help the basic problem, only the symptoms and I want the problem solved! Nevertheless, there really isn't anything else I know to do but take them; so here goes the first two.

Good news, this is the fourth "good" day I've had in succession. I even got weak and 'burnt out' today from helping Mom buy groceries, but it only took me three hours of rest to recuperate and I even regained some of my strength. Anyway, I remember when I had to wait for her in the car instead of going in the store. I really think I'll make it after all! Thank God for today.

By this time, it was obvious to me that the medical profession did not have the answers I needed. I *wanted* to be well; I *needed* to be well. I was aware that the hope I had in the doctors and the medicine was false and completely unfounded, yet I still was not willing to discard any possibility, no matter how far fetched it was. I needed desperately to find the key to my treasure—to my health—and I didn't know exactly where to look. I had begun to look up for it, as I did that day; I couldn't make it back home on my own, yet I didn't want to overlook any other possible avenue. So until I had succeeded in finding exactly what I needed, I was not going to limit myself. I was intent upon using my every available resource in hope of finding that special key to unlock my treasure. I searched anywhere and everywhere I could in order to find my answer. I searched man, I searched that awesomely incredible force I had recently become acquainted with, and I searched within myself. I seemed to be making little, if any progress, but I continued to seek.

May 4, 1980

Today was the worst day I've had all week. The stiffness was almost incapacitating. I could barely walk and my ankles were so weak I could hardly even stand to take a shower. My central nervous system was in such a disarray that I ended up with a tension headache and that crazy tingling in my scalp for no apparent reason. That's really irritating to have a tension headache and not be tense about anything. The only thing pressing in my life right now that could possibly cause any stress is lupus. Sure that's enough to be 'stressed out' about but fortunately I'm not. Sure lupus is a pain, in every sense of the word, but that's nothing new. As a matter of fact, there are no grave new changes taking place in my life right now that could cause stress or a tension headache. Now if I had gotten a tension headache during those haphazard days of trying to find out what was wrong with my body or even during those inhuman days of the hospital, I would have understood, but things are somewhat 'normal' now; meaning that lupus is simply here now, no stranger to me, and I've even become accustomed to dealing with it to some extent; so what's there to be tense about? Not a thing; my system has just gone haywire, as usual. It's just lupus being illogical and irrational again. All I can do is pray again tonight and have faith that tomorrow will be better. The side-effects of the medicine are getting worse, so I'll be glad when I go to the doctor on Tuesday. Thank God for today.

May 5, 1980

The best way to describe me at this point is "?" I just don't know. I don't know anything anymore! I thought I was improving last week, now I'm not so sure. Today I was bombarded with a multitude of symptoms; aching groins, pain in my left shoulder, more of the rash, and of course, everyday the same old stiffness. In addition to all of that, the side effects are still getting worse. Dr. Carmine said he might cut the medicine tomorrow instead of on Tuesday. Naturally, "we'll have to wait and see" (That phrase seems to always be tacked onto the end of every sentence). So

I'm suppose to call him in the morning. But now I'm having second thoughts. The weakness is back and I don't know if I'm getting better or not. I knew I could expect all of these symptoms to return at some time or another before the disease goes into remission, but all at once, I'm not ready for this. Maybe I'm just being too impatient. It's just that I've fought so long and so hard, I'm a little tired. I thank God for today but maybe tomorrow will bring new hope.

May 13, 1980

Today's outlook was good from the start. Today was a good day for me physically and the doctor's visit was promising. He cut my dosage of prednisone to 10 mg/day instead of 15 mg/day and scheduled my next visit for two weeks instead of one. Real progress, huh? I remember when I was going to his office every day then every other day for months. I guess I am improving after all. He also told me to call Monday to check on my letter of recommendation for relocation. I praise the Lord for these blessings.

One may wonder why I did not like Ohio. Well, I had never lived anywhere other than the East Coast. I was a little naive and very ignorant of life outside my homeland. Growing up in a small peninsula town, surrounded by water, meant practically living on fresh seafood. Not only was I used to it, but I liked it. It was almost as if it was a part of me; I had never known anything else. I felt as if a part of me was missing when seafood was not a part of my diet. I also felt I was missing out on certain minerals and the like, and I did not like that. It was not only impossible to catch fresh seafood in Cincinnati, but it was impossible to even purchase it. Sounds petty, I know, but we humans are creatures of habit and generally are not too willing to change behavior patterns that we enjoy. I later understood we were inland, and no water meant no fresh catch; however, the initial cultural difference was devastating. So was the case with no beach, waterfront, or shoreline. Sure there was the Ohio River, but what was that?

The weather of the Midwest was another thing I had to adjust to. The weather in Ohio was hideous compared to that of my hometown. Winters in Cincinnati were ravaging. They were so cold that car washes closed down because the water would freeze before it could be wiped off. Car washes were not the only businesses that shut down completely; other businesses also would close their doors each evening as soon as the murky gloom of dusk appeared. There would be few, if any, businesses open after dark, and people would rush home to make it inside before the streets and steps turned to ice. There was always snow on the ground that melted only temporarily during the daylight hours, only to freeze again at sundown. This was a common occurrence, a way of life, so most businesses closed early. Human existence outside after dark was life-threatening. The temperature remained below zero, and snowfall was continuous. It would snow huge, fat, heavy flakes three or four times a day, for days and weeks on end. The year I was there, it actually snowed after Easter. It was customary to allow an extra twenty to thirty minutes in one's schedule only to clean snow off the car and dig it out before going anywhere, whether it be to work in the morning, lunch at noon, or home in the evening. All of this was a bit too much for someone coming from a climate where winters usually consisted of thirty to forty degree temperatures and a good snow fall usually measured two inches or less. What an adjustment!

During my stay in Cincinnati, I worked as a field sales representative and almost lost it when informed to be prepared with quilts and candy bars in my trunk, in the event I got stranded in the snow while making business calls. Life went on as usual in these arctic conditions; schools and jobs continued, and everyone acted as if this was normal. For them it was; for me it was simply devastating. For a moment I thought I was in Alaska or Poland or someplace!

The summers in Cincinnati were just as bad. The weather forecast was ditto every day, there was never a change. The forecast always consisted of the three H's: hot, hazy, and humid. The temperature and the level of humidity seemed to always be the synonymous figures of 92, 96, or 98. The pollution only magnified an already bad situation. Thanks to large manufacturing corporations, the sun and blue skies rarely entered one's vision. The easiest way to occupy myself while sitting in rush hour traffic was to guess who was brewing what as I passed along the way. The overwhelming smells of lemon dish washing liquid and scented toilet tissue seemed to constantly fill the air, as their plants turned the Ohio River into the perfect shade of café au lait.

All of these reasons were coupled with the fact that I felt like a complete outsider there. Generally, people on the coast are very transient. We will very readily take a three-hour drive in any given direction to venture to another city or even another state. People on the coast are always in their cars, on the train, or even on the bus, going someplace—to visit friends, relatives, or simply just to sight-see. People in the Midwest usually have to travel very long distances to reach a destination of any sort, for their part of the country is vast-ly spread out. As a result, most midwesterners never leave their lit-tle cubicle. I found that most of them are very much content never going any other place or seeing anything else. That too was a differ-ent culture than the one I was used to. On the coast, we valued diversity, change, and growth. In the Midwest they valued quies-cence. I knew that anything that did not grow, subsequently died, and I could not understand this sort of stagnation. Unfortunately, our adventurousness and inquisitiveness were disdained in their eyes.

Socially, they made me feel like an outcast. If I had not grown up with them, gone to school with them, married with them and had children with them, in their eyes, I did not belong. I saw this attitude transmitted time and time again at the many social func-tions I attended. Most of them treated outsiders as intruders. I wanted to leave!

But the worst problem I had with Cincinnati was the blatant acts of prejudice I encountered. Most Caucasians treated Blacks as if we had no intellectual ability at all, nor any common sense for that matter. Salesclerks, when they would mistakenly shortchange me at checkout counters, would act surprised if I noticed the mis-take. I knew of numerous cases of job or housing discrimination, that were never addressed.

One day while making sales calls, two Caucasian boys called me a *nigger*. Fortunately for their sakes, they fled before I had a chance to respond. Once I returned to the office, I confided in a few of my co-workers what had happened, and the African-Americans were the first to admit they did not understand why I was so upset. It was 1980, and they acted as if they were still waiting for the Civil Rights Movement of the 1960s to take place.

The Klu Klux Klan had a huge rally in the park, complete with police protection and full news coverage for publicity. I knew then it was time for me to get out of Dodge!

May 17, 1980

What a dreary day. It's been raining since yesterday non-stop. So I couldn't go for my walks today. As a result, I've really had the blahs physically and mentally. One good thing though— I finally got my head back on straight and am more determined than ever to beat lupus. I have to get my health back to continue on with my life. The symptoms haven't been too overpowering today. The stiffness was present as usual, but the only other signs I had was muscle weakness and some fatigue. That's mainly because I haven't been walking. Still no nausea, arthritis, nor palpating heart! Thank God! I pray tomorrow is not rainy.

Thank God for today!

May 25,1980

What about today—it started out real well, I felt good. Rushed trying to get ready for church and got 'burned out'. What a disappointment! Mom and I made it out to the car but I was getting weaker by the minute. So I ended up coming back in the house, spending most of the day in bed. Sometimes I wonder if I'll ever get well? But I did see improvements in other areas though; I could raise my leg high enough to put my foot in the chair while sitting today.

Thank God for little miracles.

May 26, 1980

Today has been better than yesterday. Not as good as the day before, but not as bad as yesterday either. My strength seems to be returning after the burned-out ordeal of yesterday. I'm a little depressed, I don't know if it's me, the disease, or the medicine; but I'm sure it will pass like everything else. Thank God for today.

May 27, 1980

Today is just one big question mark—again! I went to the doctor today, he's pleased with my progress and even reduced my intake dosage of steroids to 5 mg/day and 10 mg/day alternating. A few of the symptoms have returned also—again; the stiffness, the shooting pains. Ironic that the doctor's report is positive (he says I'm progressing) yet the pains still persist. I don't understand, but he does, I think, or does he? Well, he has had a lot more experience with lupus than I have. I've got to get better. I will get better. Faith must prevail!

". . . the testing of your faith worketh patience. But let patience have her perfect work, that you may be complete and entire, lacking nothing." James 1:3–4

May 31, 1980

I feel a little like myself today, we had our neighborhood cookout and I had a great time. I felt a little left out because I couldn't play volleyball with the others. I couldn't do anything else that required any type of activity either, but still by sitting in the shade, I felt pretty good. Now that sounds really strange, to feel pretty good not being able to do anything—I won't even try to explain that one.

Anyway, I think the funny feeling I had that resembled a rocking sensation must have been a tinge of a seizure of some type. Seeing that lupus has already attacked my central nervous system. Still I hope that's not the case, I don't know what I would do if I were one of those lupus patients that had convulsions.

That would really change my life. Please God have mercy on my body here on earth. Please make me well again. Amen

June 2, 1980

Although today marks another day of improvement, I still wonder how much of the battle I've actually won. The stiffness is practically gone now and my strength has almost returned. I have very little arthritic symptoms, but my hair is still coming out. I still shield myself from the sun, I wonder will I ever be normal again. Thank God for today.

June 17, 1980

Today is even better yet. The only symptom I have is a little arthritis and a little weakness. I still can't squat on my knees but today I was able to sit with one leg folded under the other, Indian-style on the floor. I couldn't help but burst into tears of joy! (smile) Things are still looking up for me even if they are slow. Thank God for blessing me!!! Thank God for today. I will win the victory yet!

At this point in my life, I didn't really know the true essence nor the true power of God. To me, God was some mystical being sitting on a throne, high above the earth's atmosphere, looking down on His creation. I guess, in a sense, He still is that, but now I know Him as a person, a people person. I know He hears prayers because I have seen Him answer mine! I feel His presence with me. I feel His peace; I feel His calmness. There's an assurance that can not be explained; yet, there is no doubt it exists, more real than life itself! Actually, it's so real that I can't logically talk myself into or out of believing it at all. No, not in the least, because it's not a belief; it is a knowing. Knowing is knowledge, and from knowledge flows wisdom. Wisdom leads to new depths of understanding, and that's where true power lies.

"Happy is the man who finds wisdom, the man who gains understanding, for she is more profitable than silver and yields better
returns than gold. She is more precious than rubies; nothing you
desire can compare with her. Long life is in her right hand; in her
left hand are riches and honor. Her ways are pleasant ways, and
all her paths are peace. She is a tree of life to those who embrace
her; those who lay hold of her will be happy."
Proverbs 3:13-18 *NIV*

June 25, 1980

Today was pretty nice. For the first time in $4^1/2$ months I was
blessed to vacuum my house, shake the rugs, and mop the
kitchen floor. Of course, I got tired and am glad the day finally
ended, but I survived with no weakness. I was even able to sit
Indian-style on the floor again tonight. That was a real surprise,
after such a hectic day. I bet it will be a surprise to the doctor too.
The only frightening thing is that I don't know if I'll be able to
do it tomorrow or not. Every day is so different, but as the saying
goes, 'let tomorrow take care of itself.'

June 26, 1980

Today was even better than yesterday, and it was the tomorrow of weakness and relapse that I feared. Thank God I'm fine!
The doctor is pleased with my progress and so am I. (finally) My
dosage of medicine is remaining the same and I'm still going to
start back to work on Monday. Mom called today and I was
blessed to share my supernatural high with her about the wonderful things that are going on here. She is such a big part of this
whole thing. It's been weeks now since she left to go back home.
I miss her so. She still encourages me and tells me not to stop
praying. Although she was with me day and night, all those
months, putting everything on hold in Newport News to wait on
me hand and foot; dressing me, bathing me, helping me in every
conceivable way, she never got tired, she never gave up—and she
never let me give up either! I miss her so very much . . . I Thank
God for my mother and for today.

Life is full of many different stages. Each stage may appear to stand alone in our minds, yet in reality, they are all delicately integrated one into another. The past influences the present, as the present eagerly yields to the future. The beautiful, interwoven fabric of personhood that we are today is only the reflection of a great process.

4. Me and Mine

Nighttime appeared as the dusk of the evening freely blended into the darkness. I noticed the fullness of the night, but I had no idea what time it really was. The sky was dark, and there was no evidence of life above the earth. As a child I could always feel life above the earth—maybe God in the heavens, maybe life on another planet, but life, nonetheless—as I would gaze up at the stars. This was different. The sky, on this particular night, was filled with a void, vacant, incomplete emptiness. *What's wrong? What happened to those other worlds*, I wondered.

As I drove down Interstate 71, it hit me. There were no lights— no lights of life above the earth, no evidence at all of the moon nor the stars. As time progressed, I came to understand it wasn't just my imagination, but the new environment I was in. Things looked different because they were different, a new place, new people, and a new life to follow.

I was determined to make my journey a success in spite of the trials that had confronted us. Our efforts to reach Cincinnati had been sharply interrupted as the engine of my newly purchased used Datsun B-610 blew six hours into the trip as we approached the Pennsylvania Turnpike. After arriving at the nearest service station, Mom and I were much astonished to find out that the only available rental car facility was another twenty miles away. Once there, courtesy of the service station attendant, we then had to drive the same distance back home again to make other arrangements to get me to Cincinnati. The flight was the only possible means of getting me to Cincinnati in time to start my new job, my first professional job in the real world.

The negative circumstances had challenged me, making me even more determined to succeed. The situation had only added fuel to my fire. Every gear had been activated, and I was now in full flight. My body and soul were at one with the 727 gliding across the sky. I wasn't sure whether the 727 was carrying me or I was carrying it.

Upon landing, the mundane duties of claiming my luggage and picking up another rental car seemed to just fall in place, and I soon found myself on my way to my new apartment. With my two new-found companions, the rented jet-red Camaro and a local street map of the area, I began another phase of my travel. I was familiar with the car, but I knew nothing about the map except it's purpose. Still, I persevered on my way.

With very little nervousness and a lot of excitement, I continued across the bridge, down Interstate 71, while simultaneously attempted to follow the markings on the map. I thought I had everything under control when, all of a sudden, I was forced to swerve the car to the right of the highway. I allowed my body to flow with the pull of the car to escape what appeared to be danger. Subsequently, onto the shoulder of the road we both went.

My brain immediately registered a loud horn, which abruptly emerged from a huge eighteen-wheeler as it zoomed by, soon appearing light years ahead of me. Catching my breath, grateful that the car and I were both still alive, I regrouped and continued on my way.

However, I didn't really understand why this person felt the need to run me off the road. I had been to big cities before, even if just to visit—D.C., New York, Chicago—and I had never seen anyone get run off the road before! *Where in the world am I,* I wondered briefly.

I did not know that trucking was big business in the Midwest. On the coast we frequently transport goods by boat; we have water. Midwesterners make big use of trucks; they have no waterways. It's a cultural thing! Whatever the reason, I didn't think the gentleman had to be that cruel. Running people off the road, in any town, was ludicrous and uncivilized in my opinion. Needless to say, this was only the first of many incidents of it's kind I experienced during my stay in the Buckeye State.

The drive from the airport was brief, so it wasn't very long before I reached my destination. It was somewhat surprising to me that I reached the apartment complex in one piece, after everything I had been through during the past forty-eight hours. Nevertheless, I had finally arrived at what was now my home away from home.

As I opened the car door to step out onto the black asphalt of the parking lot, the door of the car immediately swung back on my leg. Numerous attempts to reopen it continued to fail until I eventually gave it one big strong jolt and forcefully pushed it open wide.

I had grown up on flat terrain; this was my first real experience with hills—there's that culture thing again! Cincinnati was full of hills, so learning to effectively drive, park, and even walk on hilly terrain was definitely another struggle, but a very essential one. This, too, became one of the new norms in my life.

As I lifted my tired, tense body out of the car, I stood in the tranquility of the night air, still and motionless for the first time in days. Mom and I had worked so hard to make my move a smooth one. We had planned every detail out so very carefully and felt as if we had taken care of all the necessary particulars. Compliments of my new employer, we had gone to Cincinnati weeks in advance to find a place for me to call home.

My new apartment complex consisted of quite a few buildings, but each building had only two floors with about thirty units. I didn't particularly like highrise buildings—what if there was a fire or the elevators were out of order—so two floors were just fine with me. The fifty-year old red brick building looked pretty good. The black railings leading up the steps and the beige hallways looked as if they had just recently been painted.

I stood for a moment in the summer breeze, taking note of my new surroundings. The neighborhood appeared to have been kept quite clean and quiet. There was a little activity going on outside, but not much.

I made my way up the black-railed steps and through the heavy glass door entrance. I turned left and proceeded down the dimly lit hallway. Just a few doors down was my apartment, #25. The ugly brown doors to each individual apartment stuck out like a sore thumb; I just knew they had made a mistake. Maybe they accidentally ordered the wrong color and couldn't return it? *But that's OK*, I thought; *this is only a beginning.* Having the key in advance made it feel a lot more like home. My first apartment, how exciting! It was a childhood dream come true.

Before I realized it, I was sitting on the brown carpeted floor thinking and wondering what to do next. I had unloaded the car, and everything I had in my possession was now inside with me, my one suitcase and a shopping bag full of extras. The one plant hanging over the top of the bag drooped exactly as might be expected after the ordeals of the day. I would have been drooping, also, had I not been operating on super auxiliary power from the excess adrenaline pumping through my body. The combination of stress and excitement really had me revved up. I was finally out in the real world, on my own, stepping into the shoes of true adulthood. This was it!

I sat on the floor looking around the empty apartment. The day had been far spent, and it was almost bedtime. Instantly, I remembered I had no bed! The movers had loaded my bed, stereo, and other possessions on the truck, but the truck had not yet arrived. Of course, I was supposed to start my new job the next day, but nothing could be done until morning. So what was I to do?

I could not stay in a place where strangers could so easily peer into my private living space through the huge patio door window, which just happen to face the parking lot. I could in no way be comfortable in a place where my private home would be such a public spectacle. What could I do? I didn't have a spread, blanket, sheet, or even newspaper to cover the large window that had been so appealing to me just weeks ago when I first saw the place. Even if I did happen to have a covering, I had no hammer, nails, or tape; how would I hang it? I knew none of my neighbors and thought it was a little too late to knock on their door. I had no idea where to find a store, at least not one open this time of night. All these ideas rushed through my head. What in the world was I to do?

Things had been so hectic prior to leaving home that I hadn't considered what it would be like once I arrived. My only concern was getting here—how thoughtless. My naivete and ignorance of the real world shone forth like a bright light. Panic blocked my mode of creativity, and I couldn't seem to think clearly enough to come up with alternative solutions to my problem. I eagerly took what I thought to be the only way out, but in essence, it was just the easiest way out. I desperately felt the need for another human being at that point, so I called the one and only acquaintance I knew in town.

I had met Cindy only a few short weeks before through one of our corporate executives. We both were pawns used to meet the company's affirmative action quota. We had met at a prearranged dinner during my initial visit to the Cincinnati office. We were both graduates of the same alma mater, although at different times, and we both were to start the same new position the next day. I just knew this new acquaintance would flourish into a wonderful long-lasting friendship. Unfortunately, I soon discovered I was sadly mistaken. Nevertheless, Cindy was my only contact at the time, so I gave her a call.

Sitting on the kitchen floor with my back against the wall, I picked up the receiver of the phone and dialed Cindy's number. Thank God I had lights and a phone that was in operation. After hearing the dreadful story of my horrendously trying journey and my apartment with no necessities, she eagerly invited me over to stay with her.

Using handwritten directions, I made my way up and down the hills across town to Evans Place where Cindy lived. Her street was just as quiet as mine, but the neighborhood and Cindy's apartment were both much nicer. There were no apartment complexes and no hills on her street. Instead, there was just a nice, quiet, residential area on flat ground, similar to what I was accustomed to back home. Finding a parking space was difficult, but I was glad I had succeeded in finding the house.

Through the glass door and into the foyer I went, but was immediately forced to come to an abrupt stop. I found myself facing a very beautiful, yet very locked, mahogany security door. The foyer, no larger than a four foot square space, smelled of new paint and fresh-cut wood. I pushed the button on the intercom for apartment #6, which was my destination. In seconds, I heard a very kind voice question *Yes?*, and I quickly responded, "Cindy? It's me, Susan."

"Oh! Come on in," she invited. Momentarily, I heard a loud buzz, and the lock on the huge mahogany door to my left was released.

I anxiously started up the narrow stairway. Initially, I was impressed with the beige carpeted steps and beautifully paneled walls, but my attitude quickly changed as the steps grew steeper and steeper with each landing. What I expected to be two flights turned out to be four; each floor had two flights of stairs per landing. In essence, that made a total of six flights. The excitement I felt upon entering the building had transformed into relief by the time I reached the third floor. As each round grew higher and higher, so did my fatigue. My energy level had kept up with each activity of the day thus far, but now they all seemed to be winding down together—the day, the activities, and my body.

Finally, I reached Cindy's apartment and the top floor of the building. There she stood, my only friend, face beaming with delight and covered with a beautiful, wide smile. Her eyes sparkled and danced; as I later found, they often did when she was excited. Her yellow-hued face shone as a ready-made backdrop for her perfect, white smile still surrounded by the leftover red lipstick and blush of the day. A *friend*, I thought, *what a welcome sight.*

"Hey, girl. Come on in," she invited, yelling at me from the top landing as I struggled up the last few steps. With her in sight I made my way to her apartment. More than happy to drop the cumbersome load that had been accompanying me during the past twelve hours, I followed her through her door, around the corner, into her bedroom. Consumed with feelings of relief, I initially noticed none of my surroundings except the bedroom toward which I was aimed. "You can put your things right here," she said, pointing to the floor near the closet door. "Girl, you really did have a time, didn't you," she said sympathetically with a chuckle.

In a flash, I dropped my suitcase, the shopping bag full of extras, my satchel purse, and all the cares of the day, all at the same time. Regaining my posture and standing empty handed for the first time in what seemed like eternity, I focused on my surroundings. Picking up on Cindy's nod, I followed her out of the bedroom, back down the hallway into the living room, where I proceeded to give her a minute by minute detailed account of my gruesome experience.

As the high ceilings, beautiful hardwood floors, and interesting floor plan registered in my overloaded brain, I realized that Cindy's apartment was part of an old renovated Victorian house. It was simply breathtaking! The fireplace, the brick exposed walls, and the large bay windows yielded nothing but elegance and charm. I had never seen anything like it before. We just didn't have apartments like that back home. Newport News was a little town, not very old at all, and most of our apartments had been recently built. There was one old neighborhood in Newport News with old houses—*Old Money* they called it—but they belonged to Whites along the waterfront. My hometown in Virginia was very segregated during my childhood years, so we Blacks usually only *looked* upon dwellings of that type. Even if we had the money, they would rarely integrate their neighborhoods by allowing us to move in. But this was 1979, and Cincinnati appeared to be different. I just loved Cindy's apartment.

Cindy's decorating style really caught my eye. There was no sofa, no couch, and no old fashioned sitting chairs; instead, she had just a few director's chairs, a TV, a stereo, and a few small tables. *How stylish*, I thought, *really chic and vogue*. And inexpensive, I later discovered.

Cindy looked so relaxed in the natural habitat of her home as we talked. She sat with one foot in the orange director's chair opposite me, as she introduced me to her roommate. Karen seemed so cool in her bright, flowered shorts and t-shirt. *That's the way I want to be*, I thought to myself. I had never had my own apartment. I had never been out on my own at all. I had never lived in a big city, nor worked on a real, grown-up professional job either. This was my big chance. This was my turn! I had finally arrived!

Filled with excitement, I was ready to take on the world. Forcing myself to return to the reality of the present, I quickly rejoined the conversation at hand. We chatted for a while, then turned in for our first big day on the job.

I was just as eager to get out of the clothes that felt painted on my body as I was to lie down. I was elated at the thought of finally ending the day. Once undressed, the warm shower felt just as refreshing as any natural spring in the south of France could have, sheer delight! Cindy's bed was queen-sized, and I all but died once my body made contact with it.

Morning came in the twinkling of an eye, and it was rise and shine at the crack of dawn. God was looking out for me, even through all of my ignorance, and in that one suitcase I just happened to have one dress and one pair of dress shoes, which I had purchased just before leaving home after the truck had left with all my other belongings. Under no uncertain terms was this to be my attire for my first big day on the job.

The moving company contacted me to inform me that my belongings had not arrived due to the truckers' strike and the nationwide gas shortage that was going at that time. I still did not realize the true extent of my problem until days began to pass and my situation remained the same. I still had no clothes, no furniture, and no car in my possession. Cindy had taken me to a store, where I bought another cheap dress to get me over the hump, but my funds were almost totally exhausted. I was required to work two weeks in the hole with no pay, and I had cleaned out my savings to buy the ragged Datsun that hadn't even made it to Cincinnati in the first place. My family, small but close-knit, was pooling their resources to get my car repaired so I could have the necessary transportation for my new field job.

My family's resources were very limited. Daddy had died of cancer the summer prior to my sophomore year of college, leaving Mom and me alone. She struggled to get me through school using Daddy's insurance money and their savings to supplement the scholarships and loans. I had carelessly used my only credit card to get the extra pleasures I desired when in college, never realizing that I might need it for something more important someday. Ironic that I had worked in retail for years, always having an abundance of clothes, and now, when I needed them most, I only had two dresses and one pair of shoes in my possession. My, how life can turn on you.

Cindy was not only my ticket for a place to live, but she was also a welcomed means of transportation to and from work. It was a grave adjustment for me to depend on someone else; to depend on a stranger, well, that was even worse, but my choices seemed limited. So I did what I thought I had to do under the circumstances and asked Cindy if I could stay a little while longer.

Cindy said it was OK, but I soon discovered that it was anything but. Cindy and Karen's attitude and behavior quickly changed. The nice hospitality they had initially displayed began to cease. They were no longer considerate and thoughtful, but instead, were very unfriendly and even rude in some instances. They didn't give me a key to the place, so I could only come and go with them.

One evening, Cindy left me stranded at the job while she went out with some friends after work. Well, I got a ride to her house, but couldn't get in because Karen was not there. I waited outside the huge mahogany door for her or Karen to arrive. Six o'clock to seven wasn't too much of a wait, but seven o'clock soon turned into eight, which eventually turned into 9:45 before anyone came to my rescue. I had no means of transportation, no public bus stop nearby, and nowhere to go except my empty apartment. Going there would present another problem of finding a ride to work the next day. So I waited! Finally one of Cindy's neighbors and her husband came in. They felt sorry for me sitting on the floor of the foyer in my work clothes, so they invited me in. I had not eaten all day—that money thing again—so they offered me something to eat. They were vegetarians and offered me something I had never seen nor tasted before, but beggars aren't choosy; I welcomed it—whatever it was. Shortly after ten o'clock, Cindy came home. We heard footsteps going upstairs and caught her attention. She mildly apologized, stating that she had forgotten I didn't have a key. I had been there a little over a week. Had I overstayed my welcome already? Did they want me to leave and were too ashamed to ask? A new pattern of behavior had developed right before my eyes.

Cindy and Karen occupied the bathroom for two full hours each morning, forcing me to shower at night and use the morning light from the kitchen window to style my hair and apply makeup. No one ever cooked; breakfast consisted of a high-energy drink, and dinner was eaten out. I was not into high-energy drinks; I was a breakfast person, a food person. As a child, Mom had always fed me breakfast before going off to school. Even in college, I would make my way to the cafe for breakfast, even when my friends didn't. Breakfast seemed to help me make it through the day. So I didn't know quite how to handle this. Oh, and dinner—I just didn't have that kind of money.

Cindy seemed to get a little irritated when I would ask her to stop by the store we passed on the way home just for a pair of stockings, so I wouldn't dare mention the supermarket, being aware of her diet and all. Still, I was grateful for a place to lay my head and a towel to shower.

After a day or two, Cindy informed me that she was not used to sharing her queen-sized bed with anyone. "It's very uncomfortable for me," she explained. "I need my rest, and I can't really get it sleeping with someone else. But you are welcome to stay and sleep on the floor if you like," she offered.

Maybe that was my cue to leave, but I still had no belongings at my place—no curtains, no towels, and no dishes. I had purchased them, but unfortunately, they weren't with me. I was not accustomed to living without the bare essentials of life, so I opted for her floor over my floor. From my point of view, I had no problem sleeping on the floor at Cindy's place. At least no one could gaze into my inner world and invade my privacy. However, much to my surprise, there *was* a problem with sleeping on Cindy's floor.

The beautiful hardwood floors were gorgeous to the eye, but deadly to the body. The first night wasn't too bad, but numerous nights of laying a tired aching body on stiff hard floorboard with no cushion for rest and relaxation was murderous. I felt like I was resting on sharks' teeth each time I turned over. The aching muscles and hurting bones multiplied with each passing night. Nevertheless, I survived, for that was the name of the game— survival.

The constant calls to the moving company each day yielded no answers, and my frantic voice choking back the tears invoked no sympathy from those whom I spoke with on the other end of the line. So for weeks, I continued staying at Cindy's under the same conditions and contacted the moving company every chance I got. This new job brought with it a new culture that viewed any type of emotional display as personal weakness or loss of control over one's life. How foolish; man doesn't have control over his life, anyway. Humans can't even breath without the assistance of God's miraculous internal bodily mechanisms. Nevertheless, I tried to hide my feelings and the pressing situations in my life while simultaneously searching for my missing belongings.

One day to my surprise, the irritated voice on the other end finally replied, "The movers will be there in the morning." What a relief! I could do nothing but cry tears of joy. Things looked like they were finally going to fall into place.

My things finally arrived, but to a very changed person. I was in no way the same person that had put those things on that truck nearly a month ago. I had been forced to move away from the comforts of an easy life, surrounded by those who loved, nurtured, and supported me, to a life alone with only difficulties and hardships knocking at my door. I had come face to face with the cruel realities of life in the real world. *Is this what it's all about*, I wondered to myself.

After my things arrived, my first reaction was to be glad that it was over. I had no idea that the situations and circumstances in my life would only worsen.

The apartment which I so eagerly desired to settle into, welcomed me with an overabundance of cockroaches. At first they just made their presence known, but before long, they seemed to act as if it was more their home than mine. Before long, I knew that either

I had to leave or they did. They obviously had been there a lot longer than I had, and seniority won out! One thing about roaches in apartment complexes—unless there is a joint effort on behalf of all tenants to get rid of them, they won't go anywhere; they'll stay right there. Truly smart survivors they are; they'll just travel from one house to another, with each generation becoming more and more immune to the pesticides used to attack them. I just couldn't take it; I refused to share my living space with such creatures. I moved out in less than a month to another apartment.

This new apartment was very impressive and quite cute. It was pretty much like Cindy's; an old Victorian house, renovated and converted into individual apartment units. It was complete with high ceilings, large bay windows, exposed brick walls in every room, two fireplaces, and a huge country-style kitchen. It was an absolute dream, with only six units in the entire building and very friendly neighbors.

Little did I know that this apartment would be more than just the place I would lay my head after long workdays. As a strange and mysterious disease seized my body, my life, and my world, this unusually comfortable apartment soon became a true haven of rest. Nevertheless, prior to this entrapment, I still had the fire of excitement in my eyes and in my heart. Rationalizing the entire moving episode by reasoning that I had just gotten off to a rocky start, I persisted with great optimism. In my heart, I truly believed things were going to get better, but the nightmare only continued.

The first landlord was very displeased about my moving out and breaking my lease, so he attempted to sue me. He falsely accused me of damages to the apartment, erroneously charging me hundreds of dollars. He sent threatening letters to my home, made harassing phone calls to my job, and followed it all up with a designated court date. After speaking with me by phone, he soon realized that I would stand up for my rights, something I found most Blacks in this new town usually did not do, so he dropped the charges and sent me a letter of apology.

Although I was greatly relieved, I could still feel the stress compounding. Weeks passed as I began to enjoy my apartment and my life again, dismissing the negative memories of the old and starting anew.

Much to my surprise again, something else was going on. I began to notice little red spots on my calves and ankles. They itched something terrible, although there didn't appear to be any sores. Soon, I discovered that this new apartment that was so pleasing to the eye had a hidden problem. It was flea infested! Little critters from the previous owner's dog had laid eggs in the floorboards. They had now hatched and wanted to call my home their home. It took three exterminations to destroy them all! I felt dirty for weeks.

These experiences only perpetuated the already unfortunate state of culture shock I found myself in as I struggled to desperately adjust to the newness of a different world.

No more hanging out with only those of my own gender, my own race, or my own interests. I was now a full-fledged member of the working class. I had to learn to play the role if I was to survive in this new world. Although somewhat ill-equipped, I managed to fit in as a Yuppie, learning as I went along. Yes, learning—learning it all, even down to eloquently eating cherry tomatoes and responding to *Hi, how are you?* each morning with a smile and a *Fine*, even when my world was falling apart!

Although that in itself was a challenge, it didn't stop there. Oh, no! The expensive lunches I could not afford, the political games I didn't approve of, and the cheerful facade that did not portray the real me only ignited more flames under a brewing pot of overwhelming frustrations. The pent up stress of it all eventually erupted and, no doubt, played a vital part in the illness that soon consumed my life.

5. Wicker Wise

Back home again. It had been two years since I left. It should feel like a repeat—returning home with Mom, giving up my apartment in the city, renting the truck, putting my furniture in storage, leaving the job under disability status—but it's not the same. It just doesn't feel like a repeat to me; no déjà vu here. Same circumstance, same situation, same place, but something is different; the time is different!

To everything there is a season, and a time to every purpose
    under the heaven:
A time to be born, and a time to die;
A time to plant, and a time to pluck up that which is planted;
A time to kill, and a time to heal;
A time to break down, and a time to build up;
A time to weep, and a time to laugh; A time to mourn, and a
    time to dance;
A time to cast away stones, and a time to gather stones together;
A time to embrace; and a time to refrain from embracing;
A time to get, and a time to lose; A time to keep, and a time to
    throw away;
A time to tear, and a time to sew;
A time to keep silence, and a time to speak;
A time to love, and a time to hate;
A time of war, and a time of peace.
Ecclesiastes 3:1–8

Time or timing, is undoubtedly one of the most, if not *the most* influential singularly acting force in our universe. All other conditions could be in place and all contingencies thoroughly well-planned, but if the timing isn't right, then all other efforts will be fruitless.

The element of time is an extraordinary force. It is totally unparalleled by any other and has a strength and a power all its own. The element of time, although totally intangible and frequently unexplainable, has built-in ability—some sort of centrifugal force, whereby it can cause change in a circumstance or in a course of action by simply *being*.

We often hear expressions like *time heals all wounds* or *it will get better with time*. Although we may feel disheartened when these words of encouragement are offered, they do have some validity. Time truly is an incredible influence.

We've all heard of living each day as if it's your last, commonly known as taking one day at a time. Let's try rearranging our vision and view life from a totally different perspective. If this were the last day of your life, what kind of choices would you make? What kinds of things would you be doing?

Many people who find themselves facing death through illness frequently ask the doctor, "How much time do I have?" Some attempt to fulfill all their earthly desires. Some decide to search themselves to determine what is really important to them. Some attempt to get in right standing with their Creator.

Why can't we or why don't we live our lives like this each day? Is it because of our society? Has our society brainwashed us into focusing only on the future, setting long-term goals and aiming only for what others identify as secured futures, never acknowledging that these desired futures may not be the best futures, nor will they necessarily always turn out the way we plan? There must be a balance. We must plan, provide, and aim for the future, while still focusing on the importance of the present, acknowledging still that there is much more that what we can see. Let us focus on that day—the only given day, the good in that day and the fruits of that day—not only waiting on the fruition of the future.

Each minute is only a temporary phase—simply a time in space that is sure to drift, fleet, or possibly even drag on, but move on just the same. It will move on to be only a memory of the past, planting a new seed for the future, while still vanishing from the present reality.

Of course, change can take place in a fleeting second, but what is truly amazing are the repercussions that can flow from the accumulation of these seemingly innocent seconds. The fleeting seconds soon turn into minutes, as the accumulation of these minutes yield to hours; they are easily translated into days. These days, unpretentious as they may seem, carry the weight and possibility of the future. They cause seasons to change, metals to corrode, children to grow up, and adults to grow old. The element of time can change people, places, and literally all things upon the face of the earth. We may watch the sweeping titter-tatter of the second hand on the clock and seldom realize its true significance. Nothing and no one can stand up against the effects of time and not be changed.

And who is the master of this powerful force called *time*? Who is held responsible for the creation of such a powerful persuasion? None other than the Creator of Life Himself. Yet, we as humans are often taught to control, manipulate, speed up, and even sometime change the course of it, disregarding the wisdom and necessity of its natural progression. What do we hope to accomplish? Are we really wiser than our Creator?

Looking back over the passage of time in my life, I see some great changes. Some I controlled, and some of which I could not control at all.

Control, or the lack thereof, is another issue that seems to plague mankind. We are conditioned by society at a very early age to be in complete control of ourselves and our circumstances at all times. We are constantly taught that we are the masters of our destinies and the captains of our ships. We are told that the world is within our reach; we can have anything we want, if we only work hard enough for it. It all sounds oh so good, but is it really true? Does this absolute statement hold total validity for all persons regardless of who you are? I presuppose that it does not.

Not to rain on your parade—nor to plant negative seeds of pessimism where optimism and positivity may breed, but it's only natural, right, and proper to present the other side of the coin. Reality, as it stands for quite a number of people in this world, is not always like that. Contrary to popular belief, there are some who are undoubtedly victims of circumstances in their lives through no choice of their own. There are those who are chosen instead of having the option to choose! True, there are some who are chosen by God to do a work, a particular task in the earth. Some are chosen to share the message of hope that, *with God, all things are possible.*[1] Some have the message of sheer survival or endurance that, *through Christ, we can do all things.*[2] Sometimes they may be the crippled, the paraplegic or the blind of our society.[3] Sometimes they may even be the homeless on the corner. They are in our societies today; they can come from any walk of life, in any town, state, or country in our world. There were numerous accounts of these people recorded in the Bible.[4]

Obviously there are some situations that may, unfortunately, suppress us or oppress us for a period of time for a given purpose, as with the blind man recorded in Saint John, Chapter 9. But here again, *time* is the main factor.

Sometimes there are situations where persons may have no available choice of action at their disposal, except to simply stand and endure. We're all probably familiar with the term *seeing the light at the end of the tunnel.* Well, sometimes there can be situations in our lives where we can't see even a flicker of light at the end of the tunnel. There are some situations wherein one is not sure that there even is a tunnel. There are no apparent boundaries, just a deep, dark space. It's evident that it's a hole because there's space up above, but you're not sure how to get out, or if an opening exist

[1] Saint Mark 10:27

[2] Philippians 4:13

[3] Saint John 9:1–7; Acts 14:8–10; Saint John 5:5–9

[4] Hebrews 11:32–38

at all. This is the true definition of *the pits*. This type of situation identifies a definite and distinctive kind of loss of control.

Usually, individuals suffering from oppressive situations fall into one of two categories: loser or winners. To the outsider, the winner may seem to be the one who has succeeded in adapting to a given situation—until the change comes—however long that may be. Some may look on and say things like, "My, he's a strong person" or "My how she's overcome," but has the person really overcome? On what basis was the judgement being made? Was it simply because the person did not give up or give in? Is that the basis upon which we make such statements? Do we believe the person has overcome simply because they kept up the fight? Is that what constitutes a winner? On the other hand, some may feel that one has only won when there is no longer a fight.

We must understand that success comes in degrees, and so does control, or lack thereof. We must be careful when judging others and their situations. We must understand the important role that extenuating circumstances may play.

Although we all may not have actually lost control of our lives, we all may have at some point felt as if we have. It is important that we distinguish the difference between what is and what we feel. Perceptions can make us think and feel all kinds of things. We may see a situation as completely hopeless or dim. That may not be the case at all. The true reality of a perception can only be determined by the actual facts surrounding the given circumstance. So many times, the true facts are very much beyond our grasp if we lean to our limited carnal thinking; subsequently, we find ourselves yielding to misconceptions about the situation. We must be very careful.

Ordinarily, we can, with effort—sometimes a little, sometimes a lot—change our perceptions, our attitudes, or behavior, and subsequently, our circumstances. But sometimes we can not. Some circumstances or conditions are destinies, our fate, that must transpire as part of the plan—the Master Plan. What does the person in the middle of that plan do?

God grant me the serenity to accept the
things I can not change,
the courage to change the things I can,
and the wisdom to know the difference.

It starts with separating the control of self from the control of
one's life. Although we may not have control over all the circumstances in our lives at all times, we do *always* have control
over how we respond to those circumstances. Responding in a
positive way to them may require little effort and be quite easy to
do, if one can clearly see that response as having a rewarding
effect. But if it is evident that no change at all will occur, that a
particular response to a given situation will undoubtedly have no
effect at all on that situation, then from where does the incentive
to fight come? How does one muster enough determination and
inner-strength to fight, knowing the outcome of one's situation
will not change?

Behavior modification, even when positive change is immi-
nent, requires some mental exercise of mind over matter and some
spiritual exercise of faith. I've learned that situations that have no
promise of change require the same techniques—however, with
much more effort and quite intense concentration.

If by chance you find yourself to be one of those chosen few
whose circumstances transcend the typical norm of disappointment, discontentment, or distress, and somehow filter into the true
realm of helplessness, threatening your basic needs of survival and
your life, what do you do? Where do you go? How do you deal?
Where do you get the necessary strength, courage, perseverance,
and power to fight what would appear to be a losing battle?

The answer is: the Creator of Life. Not to be taken as simply
a religious answer, this is the only valid response to such an overwhelming question. Whether examined logically, rationally, spiritually, or even scientifically, what better source is there than the
source from which a thing is derived? There is none! Therefore,
it follows to say, if man's life is threatened by any uncontrollable

circumstance and one needs to rise above it, the only feasible solution by which one may do this is to go to a higher source, the main source, the source of all creation: God.

The next question one may ask is, "Who is God?" God Jehovah; Almighty God; El Shaddai; God of Abraham, Isaac, and Jacob; Susan's God; Adon; the Great I Am; El Elyon; Elohim; Adonai; Elah; or Yahweh. No matter what one wishes to call Him, there is only one God—the force behind all creation.

As to whether God is a he, a she, or an it, depends strictly on what your source of information is. If your source is the Holy Scriptures of the Bible handed down through hundreds of generations, if your source is this same Word of God as first written in Hebrew and Greek on papyrus by the great Prophets, if your source is the same Spirit of Christ that promises to manifest Himself to them that obey this same Word as recorded in Saint John 14:21, then you are speaking of the same God of Israel as I am, and that God is a He.

On the other hand, if you are of the New Age persuasion or believe in other doctrines and other gods derived from various religions—Egyptology and the like—then you are tampering with the spirit of the anti-Christ! Since the beginning of time, the Egyptians never believed in the God of the Israelites, nor the God of the Bible; that's what the story of Moses and the Red Sea is all about. As the signs of the times tell us, we are approaching the end of this age, and the spirit of the anti-Christ has been loosed in the earth for such a time as this. The spirit of the anti-Christ, also known to be the spirit of the devil, wishes to take captive all that he can, so as to rob them of the abundant and everlasting life that God has planned and offered to all mankind through his Son, Jesus the Christ. So many times we are deceived to the point that we can even accept the fact that there is the spirit of the anti-Christ in the earth today, but cannot accept the fact that the Spirit of Christ is in the earth. Now, how much sense does that make? How can you have an *anti* to something or someone you say does not exist? Reader, beware! Satan's main tool is that of deception! So I admonish you, don't be quick to follow religions that you know so little or nothing about. Beware of what god you choose or serve!

Some may focus on the big bang theory. Some may even believe in the theory of evolution. Both of these technically address the issue of development instead of creation. I choose not to belabor this point with argument or debate; however, I will pose the questions to you science buffs: where do you think the force of the big bang came from; who created the ape?

When traced back, anything and everything is derived from *something*. If traced far enough it will eventually lead to a core, which will lead to it's source—so it would be with these theories—and the source of these and all other creations is, of course, God, and God alone.

6. Contrast and Candor

The refreshing, rejuvenating shower that seemed so appetizing in thought soon became a nightmare in reality. Knees swollen twice their normal size, I wondered if it was the disease or the medicine. My legs felt as if steel rods had replaced the bones, and the arthritic pains seemed to scream out for attention. Still, the warm water felt unbelievably comforting to my stiff body! With legs a little weak and ankles very shaky, I attempted to enjoy the relaxing sensation of the warm water running down my frame. Soaking in the tub would have been a real treat had kneeling to get in and out been possible, but not this time. The mere thought of difficulty in cleaning the tub afterwards left very little room for contemplation of the matter.

I concentrated on the warm feeling—water truly does have a calming effect. I stood still as I allowed it to run down my upper torso, trying desperately to ignore the stiffness in my legs that seemed to be increasing by the minute, while the tension surrounding my neck and shoulders undoubtedly ceased. The emotional side of my brain sent persuasive messages for me to stand there all night and enjoy the feeling, but the left side of my brain quickly interrupted with logic and reasoning, as it sent signals of warnings that my task would prematurely be interrupted by discomfort if I didn't hurry.

First a soapy lather! *Umph, where did that come from?* I wondered. While attempting to wash my back, an unexpected muscle spasm had forced me to stop my stroke midstream. I had been using my left hand to do the job, but now to my dismay, I was forced to use my right hand. My right arm barely had enough strength to lift itself, much less accomplish the task of washing my entire body. Nevertheless, I focused all of my energies on the job before me, and through various methods of maneuvering, I was able to succeed. To my surprise, I had soon worked my way down to my lower torso. Last but not least, came the job of lifting my legs to wash my feet. Boy, was I glad I hadn't worn sandals.

Legs strong enough to support me, allowing me to stand and balance my body weight—what a blessing! My legs did not *have* to move at all. My muscles did not *have* to lift my arm, nor did my brain *have* to send the proper messages to other parts of my body to function appropriately. Neither do yours! These are all blessings given to us by the grace of God, not to be overlooked and definitely not to be taken for granted.

Good health is the norm for most people in our society. Most of us have it and always will have it. We hurriedly go on with our daily lives, rarely thinking that there are others who don't. We rarely stop to think how fortunate we really are. We seldom realize that there are others confined to wheelchairs—some who have never walked a step in their lives and still others who have no control over *any* of their body functions. Sure, we know these people exist. We may see them on the street, in hospitals, on TV, even some in the Special Olympics, but do we ever really stop to think what life for them is really like? How they must feel to be incapacitated? What about the issues of self-pride and dignity in their lives? Do they exist, and to what degree?

My mind's eye quickly travels back to an encounter I had with a patient at one of the greatest learning medical centers in the country.

I see myself walking down the brightly lit hallway of the second floor with my vision blurred by tears. The feeling of total isolation seemed to overwhelm me as I began a dialogue with myself. *This is so unfair! All I wanted to do was walk her to the elevator. I'm really fed up with this! Enough is Enough!* I was so angry I didn't know what to do. I continued to protest as I slowly walked down the hall back to my room.

Mom had come to visit with me for a little while. Visiting hours were now over, and it was time for her to leave. "Why couldn't I have at least walked her to the elevator," I whimpered.

I felt the frustration building up on the inside; I wanted so desperately to lash out at something, someone, anything, anyone. Who was to blame for the state I was in? Who's fault was it that my legs ached and my body was too weak to barely carry me? Who should I be angry with? The wells of water overflowed in my eyes, and before I could stop them, the tears had come rolling down my cheeks like a huge waterfall.

At that very instant, I heard Rose's voice call out to me. Her familiar sparkling smile was happily dancing along the backdrop of her pale, white-skinned face. Her shoulder-length hair had been combed, but not styled. Her home-made dress, unmade face, and brown hair, all seemed to just blend in together, leaving front stage to her comforting smile and transparent brown eyes. Rose had very unusual eyes, the kind that seemed to simply penetrate one's soul and deposit a great big chunk of love there. Her eyes pieced mine as they attempted to dilute the anguish I was feeling.

She interrupted my deep sense of concentration and intense mood of self-pity as she bluntly asked, "How do you that?"

I looked up in surprise and sharply responded, displacing all of my anger and despair onto the first person to cross my path, "How do I do what?" I asked to what she was referring just to be polite. Deep down inside I really didn't care. I was so wrapped up in my situation that nothing else really mattered. The only thing I knew was that I was upset! I wanted my situation to change, and I felt helpless. I hated the condition I was in. I wanted to be well! So, still consumed with the idea of *me*, I continued to quarrel within myself as I waited for Rose to reply.

Rose's answer immediately penetrated my thoughts as she shocked me with her response. "That . . . *walk!*" Her words rang out loud in my consciousness, reeling me in from my deep sea of depression and despair. In my silence, she went on to explain that she had been wheelchair-bound all her life and had always wondered what it would feel like to balance oneself and actually walk. I can still hear her voice ever so clearly as she ended her quest for understanding by innocently asking, "Aren't you afraid you'll fall?"

I had been so preoccupied with my little world that I had missed the larger picture—I could not see the forest for the trees. I had been so consumed with my pain and discomfort that I had failed to acknowledge that it could be worse. I could at least move. Painful as my limbs were, I still had them, and they were alive enough to actually feel the pain and be mobile.

My outward response was pure silence, as the loud bell of reality rang out in my head. It was as if I had been in a deep sleep and, surprisingly, the alarm had gone off. I was so very sure that my problem of pain was legit; I was convinced that what I was going through was ultimate in the realm of suffering, but then there was Rose. Her case was much different from mine and, yes, much worse. She had *never* walked at all and probably never would. Rose had spina bifida, so the lower portion of her body never properly developed. She had spent the entire thirty-six years of her life in a wheelchair!

I felt as if someone had just thrown a bucket of ice cold water in my face and awakened my senses. I attempted to regain my composure. How could she throw me for such a loop so easily with just one simple question? How could I have been so blind and ignorant to overlook the sheer miracle of walking, even if for a moment?

I began to reminisce about where God had bought me from. My memory was quickly jarred back in time to the period when I couldn't walk; how could I have forgotten? How could I have forgotten so easily how it felt not to be able to function? I had been there! The sobering fact of the true insignificance of my preoccupation with self simply left me dumbfounded.

I was speechless in response to such a basic, simple, and yet so complicated question. I did not know how to exactly answer Rose. How do you explain to someone how to walk? Something seemingly so very easy to do, yet so complex.

We are often aware that situations of this nature exist, but few of us ever actually experience them. If the experience has not been a personal one, then it may be difficult for one to have a true appreciation for the magnitude of such limitations. For clarification, I would like to suggest a very brief exercise that just might foster a greater understanding of such.

94

For the next few minutes, sit still in a comfortable position, in a quiet environment, and do the following:

1) Close your eyes.

2) Envision yourself getting dressed.

3) Visualize your every move.

4) Imagine each action of every step.

5) Visualize your bodily movements as you put on each article of clothing.

6) Concentrate closely as you see yourself lifting your legs, your arms, and by all means, don't forget to balance yourself.

Pay close attention to every aspect of your motions as you move your arms forward, backwards, and up. Do you use your fingers to button your buttons? Is flexibility of your fingers needed to zip a zipper? Don't forget the energy that is required, and coordination is a must. Acknowledge how each muscle has its own function, serves its own purpose and, yet, can in no way complete any task without the help of its friends, the other connective tissues— the tendons, ligaments, and bones. OK, Let's try the exercise. Ready? Begin!

So many of us take these things for granted, never really paying attention to the complexities involved in our daily activities of normal survival tasks. However, there are some who put forth extra effort each day to do the simplest of things.

Shortly after my second return to my hometown, I ran into an old friend—an older gentleman mind you, retired from the military, and a real aggressor who was successfully self-employed. He said to me, "What are you doing these days?"

I responded, "Oh, I'm writing a book and recuperating from a recent bout of illness." He was aware of my situation with lupus.

We joked around as the conversation flirted on to other topics, then again he asked, "So, what have you been doing since you've been back home, nothing?"

I had already answered the question once, but I guess my first response was not sufficient for him; he thought if he rephrased it, my reply might change. In his mind, if I wasn't engaged in what some call gainful employment, then I guess I was doing nothing. Ah, so is the mentality of most in our society.

Unfortunately, some people must work for physical survival instead of financial gain! For some, the bodily motions visualized in the previous exercise do not come easy. Some work very hard at simple things, like using the toilet, eating a meal, or getting dressed.

During the seven years I lived with this so-called incurable connective tissue disease, I worked harder than I would have worked on anyone's job, mentally or physically.

We must grow to have an appreciation for all types of work and all types of struggle, not only in the workplace, but outside as well—personal and public. All struggles, regardless of the type, require hard work, dedication, and determination. The setting or the goal may be different, but the formula for success is always the same. Let not our minds become so small that we can only see our little world. Others may not be where we are mentally, physically, or spiritually.

March 25, 1983

Well, here we go again. Dr. Sykes looked at me today with grave concern. He said, "We have to do something!" I'd been battling all week, or was it two, with severe skin problems. Increased steroids and cortisone creams didn't do any good—so what now? The dermatologists are at a loss too. Dr. Sykes fears sepsis will set in, since some of the lesions are emitting puss. Much to my dismay, I agreed to go to one of the larger medical colleges upstate. So I'm going to be a guinea pig once again. I hate that—but what else can I do?

My family is so supportive. Mom is like a second skin—always there! I pray God bless and reward her for all her many forms of love.

We left Dr. Sykes' office to go to the mall. It was so hard to find some decent sleepwear. Usually the choices are so plentiful that they're overwhelming, but not this time. We could hardly find anything nice. As soon as we got back home, the hospital called to say the bed was ready. We called Aunt Evelyn and Aunt Shirley, and they immediately came out to the house. From that point on it was total chaos. Mom hemmed my new robe, Evelyn ironed all my things, and Shirley helped me pack; talk about teamwork. By now I've started with more symptoms: dizziness, nausea, diarrhea, and extreme fatigue. Fear soon began to set in just thinking about going to Clarkston.

I'd never been to Clarkston before, and I don't know anyone living in that area. So I guess I won't have any visitors. Visitors always help during hospital stays. Weeks ago, my spirit told me I would take a trip to a place that began with a C and that I would be so much better when I returned, but I had no idea it would be Clarkston. What frightens me the most is the feeling I have that I'll be there for a while. That's why I'm praying so very hard. I pray that God stays very close by my side and lets me know that He's still there. I'm a baby Christian, and I need lots of reinforcement to keep my faith from wavering. He's so merciful that He's doing just that. I feel His Spirit all around me. Thank God for being LOVE!!!

Renee and Lizzy came over to visit before I left. I cried a little—I really don't know why; sadness, fear, joy, a little of all, I guess. Judith and Becky gave me words of encouragement as usual, and I was almost on my way. Evelyn and Shirley didn't leave until 12:00 midnight. Mom and I took our baths to get some sleep—we were going to leave at 6:30 A.M. Of course, I was so worked up that I couldn't sleep. I finally got to sleep around 3:00 A.M. I didn't let Mom know though because she's been running so much helping me; I wanted her to get some rest. I laid there thinking 5:30 would never come. Well, it finally did and I was glad to get the show on the road. My Aunt Martha was here, too, tonight as we prepared things; she tries so hard to make things easier for Mom and me.

So daylight broke; she, my Uncle Bora, my mom and I left for Clarkston. I had more symptoms but I didn't really care; I just wanted to get there and get it over with.

March 26, 1983

I had enough energy to get dressed and thank God my stomach accepted breakfast. I couldn't eat much but it was a big improvement since my appetite had been so poor all week. Thank God I didn't even get diarrhea afterwards. Aunt Martha came over again this morning to see if we needed anymore help and we were on our way. Family support is so special and so important.

By the time we arrived, 10:30 A.M., I was really weak and tired from so little sleep. The admitting process took over an hour; then it all started.

They transported me to another building across the street called the *Twin Building*, on the second floor, to a private room. The building here is very old, the halls are narrow, and the rooms are extremely small. There is a tiny little black and white TV and no private shower. I know it sounds as if I expect a five-star hotel or something; I don't. I've just been spoiled by fancy modern hospitals. Nevertheless, I prayed over this upon my arrival, and God told me *this is best*! That familiar voice again and that reassurance deep down on the inside. I don't know why but He says, "Don't worry about it," so I'm gonna listen to Him and trust His judgement; He knows a lot more than I do. I really don't know how long I'll be here though; this room is $96 more a week than the semi-private. They're letting Mom stay in here for right now on a cot.

Thank God again! I've been praying for her peace and contentment. She's so sacrificing. Luckily her appetite has been good, and I think she needed the rest from waiting on me at home, ripping and running all the time. Here she has to sit still for a while and let the nurses do some of the work. Strangely enough by the end of day 1, the room had grown on me and I have decided to totally forfeit the idea of switching to a semi-private one, even though the phone in here is temporarily out of order. That was my only contact back home. But anyway . . .

They didn't waste any time with treatment. Medical student Sam came in before I could get undressed. He took what looked like a pint of blood—he said he wanted 25cc's but settled for 23cc's because my vein collapsed. It hurt really bad. I cried; then I got extremely weak. They finally fed me. Lunch was good for hospital food—spaghetti and broccoli—or maybe I was just famished. (smile)

After lunch, more doctors came by—a resident and an intern. They had laundry lists of questions as they examined me. It was OK though; the medical profession need all the help they can get. They don't know much about lupus; it really baffles them, so if I can help then that's OK. They were very nice, with good bedside manners. They spent quite a bit of time with me doing examinations including an EKG which came out negative. Soon the day was over and it was night. Mom rolled my hair; they gave me this medicine for my mouth ulcers, a sleeping pill, and it was all over.

God bless!

March 27, 1983

Breakfast was served at 8:00 A.M. so we didn't sleep late—you never can in the hospital. We had planned to go to the 4th floor to Baptist (not that it mattered) Church Service at 10:00 but a team of five (5) doctors came in right after breakfast to talk to me some more. We discussed alternative methods of treatment for lupus, other than steroids. By the time they left and I showered, I was too weak to go to the service, so back to bed I went for more rest and a nap. The meals today were OK and so was my health. A bit of weakness and bouts of fatigue, but all and all, it was an OK day.

They started a 24 hour urine collection. We're going to bed early tonight because tomorrow promises to be quite busy with a lot of doctors coming by bright and early, so I'm told, possibly all day long, and how could I forget—more blood to be drawn.

Oh! I did meet some other patients on the floor today. God sent one very special woman from down the hall since I was sad about missing the church service. She visited for a while and we shared testimonies of the love of God and what He has done in our lives. She thinks she has cancer of the gall bladder, but the doctors are reluctant to operate. She really wants to know for sure what's wrong with her. I know the feeling. Sometimes it's worse not knowing. I pray God gives her answers and peace, she was really a sweet and loving person. Two other patients came to visit tonight, too. Both men sick for six (6) years with skin diseases; one had a terrible case of psoriasis, the other had scleroderma. There are so many sick people in the world. I wonder why????

Well, it's about 9:00 P.M. and we're getting ready for bed. I'm gonna roll my hair and call it a night.

Thank God for all His blessings. G-Nite!

March 28, 1983

Today was even worse than I imagined. I didn't get to sleep until after 11:00 P.M. last night and was up at 6:30 A.M. Unfortunately, my body is like that of an infant these days and that just wasn't enough sleep. Still groggy, I took a shower. As soon as I arrived back to my room, the 'big man' was here, Dr. Dean, the rheumatologist Dr. Sykes had referred me to. All the other little peons are under him. He was very nice and appeared to be more knowledgeable than most about lupus. He spent about $1/2$ hour with me, then breakfast came, of course before he left so it got cold. And how could I have forgotten the blood technician who came before breakfast taking six (6) tubes again. Anyway, they finally left and I tried to eat the cold breakfast and took a nap. Mom went to run some errands and as soon as she returned, it all started.

With no warning, they woke me up to go across the street to the eye clinic. I jumped out of bed, even when I knew it wasn't in my best interest to do so, and rushed to go with them, only to be there in the clinic for three (3) hours. Boy, were there examinations extensive; they did it all. After all the pain, burning, and discomfort from the exam, they didn't even give me any shades to put on. I had to travel back to my room with the blanket over my head to shield my eyes from sunlight. The discomfort is just leaving now and it's about 8:00 at night. Since the eye clinic ordeal today, I've seen other doctors, eight (8) to be exact.

The dermatologist put me in quarantine today because of the lesions. They act like they are trying to protect themselves, but I'm the one needing the protection! I'm not contagious, but my low resistance to infection makes me feel as if they have something I can catch, and they do—germs. Hospitals are the easiest place to pick up unwanted germs. Anyway, it was a very stressful and disappointing day being isolated from the rest of the world.

Thank God all the tests results have come back OK thus far. The eyes are A-O.K., no glaucoma nor cataracts, both of which are to be expected from the extensive steroid therapy I've had over the past few years. Nevertheless, the doctors are somewhat concerned about my kidneys spilling protein and will decide later about doing a biopsy. All and all I'm still trying to trust in God. Hoping tomorrow will be even better. I did receive my first telephone call today. Deidra called from D.C.; she really brightened by night.

God bless Mom & everyone . . .

March 29, 1983

My day—Happy Birthday to me! And what a way to celebrate a birthday—not only miles away from family and friends, but in the hospital, what a trip! But still it was a beautiful day. Mom was here again, as usual. I received four (4) bouquets of flowers and some cards today. Mom came through with balloons, and God sent me a special friend named Bobby, who works at the florist. He seems like a very nice person. All and all it was OK. I also received long distance calls from Judith, Becky, Patricia, Patty, Marcy, and my aunt Evelyn. The Woodwards sent flowers, so did my family from home, and the new friend Bobby brought by a special bouquet, also.

The doctors' visits weren't too bad today. Dr. Dean came by with some other doctors and students, they even took some pictures of my hands. He seems so very knowledgeable, professional, honest, and yet compassionate. No new news except to schedule a nephrologist, and then possibly a kidney biopsy.

Mom has gone to the hospitality house. That's really a blessing for her. She gets a chance to leave this depressing hospital and go to another environment—a much nicer, more home-like environment with other people who are here with their loved ones going through similar experiences. It's very much like a Ronald McDonald House, and very 'comfortable', so she says.

You run across such freak illnesses here. I call it the 'Freak Zoo' because doctors send their patients here when they don't know what else to do for them or how to treat them anymore. Looking around the place really puts life in a new perspective; people with cancer six or seven times and Rose with spina bifida (36 years old and never been able to walk) . . . that's a whole new realm of reality.

I'm more than ready to turn in; it's 10:00 P.M. and these 6:30 A.M. mornings are killing me. (smile) Today wasn't too bad; God renewed my strength, once again. I saw a few of the fruits of my labor today by talking with the medical social worker and nurse about the emotional aspects of chronically ill patients. They were very impressed and pleased with the positive way in which they say I have dealt with my situation. I know it is only the Lord that has gotten me through and I told them that. I don't know what tomorrow will hold; neither do the doctors. They aren't even sure what direction to take, so I'm praying harder than I've ever prayed before. We all need knowledge, wisdom, and direction. I need strength, courage, and faith. I know God is with me and I've put things in His hands just as I have so many times before, but this time I'm forced to leave them there and hold on tighter to His hand than ever before—and I do mean tight!

Oh! In honor of my birthday today, the Dietary Department sent up a large cupcake and the nurses sang *Happy Birthday* to me—wasn't that cute? (smile) Well, that's it. May God bless everyone—including me.

G-Nite, Love Susan

March 30, 1983

Well, today was a lot brighter, just like the card the Lupus Group sent from home. The dark days of discouragement were only a forerunner of the brighter days to come. The flowers, cards, and calls yesterday set the stage and pace for the flow of

God's love. He knew how much I disliked this dull, drab place and He did something to change it. I got past the 'red tape' today, through to the 'head honcho' of the Infectious Disease Control Center and succeeded in getting the isolation rules lifted. Thank God for little things.

Being in isolation was a big emotional strain so God brought a rainbow that way. Bobby came by again today and we shared a very long and fulfilling conversation on faith, spirituality, and God's purposes. That was a big blessing for us all. Mom's experience with the hospitality house is running very smoothly; she seems to be very content there, at least as much as possible under such circumstances.

The doctors didn't let up today either. Although Dr. Woodman came by this morning before breakfast, he also came by on four (4) other separate occasions. In addition, the dermatologist asked for my permission to bring some students by to learn more about lupus. I agreed and he showed up with seven (7). I should have charged them an admission fee. (smile)

After that came the nephrologist team to discuss my kidneys. First one came, then he left and came back with others. We discussed the possibilities of treatment more and the biopsy procedure. We sure do a lot of discussing! (I guess that's good, I wouldn't want to be ignorant or left out) They stayed for about 45 minutes. The 'leader of the pack' said they would 'prep' me for the biopsy by checking my clotting time. "The prevention of hemorrhaging is essential," he says. Then the chemotherapist came in to discuss the pros and cons of Cytoxin, an anti-cancer agent. As a finale, Dr. Dean—the big man—came in to confirm the course of action. The biopsy will be done on Friday.

I got a few long distance calls tonight from friends and relatives. All and all, I see the manifestation of God's Spirit in so many ways. The doctors seem to be very thorough, cautious, and caring. That's one thing I can say, every since I've been going through this with lupus, God has always blessed me with the very best health care possible. I thank Him for that!

It's almost unbelievable how much knowledge God has given man about the human body; it's incredible. The doctors now have the direction I've been praying for and so do I; we're going to go with the biopsy. I also have the peace and faith that only God can give.

I met three other ladies in the lounge tonight and saw God use me to manifest the purpose of my life 'in the land of the living'. Praise His Holy Name! Praise the all-powerful God of heaven and earth! "Those that wait upon the Lord shall have renewed strength."

I don't know what tomorrow holds, but I do know who holds the key and who runs the show . . . and He's on my side! G-Nite.

March 31, 1983

What a trip day! It's 8:00 at night and I am lying here with a heplock in my right arm which prevents me from writing. My vein is very sensitive and vulnerable; I'm afraid to be too active with that arm, for fear that it'll collapse like it has so many times before. Mom is sweet enough to record this for me. The kidney biopsy is scheduled for 8:00 A.M. tomorrow morning; today they took me through the ringer and 'prepped' me.

The blood technician arrived before breakfast—again. I was up at 2:00 A.M. with diarrhea, chills, and nausea, so my entire night's rest was severely broken; that, of course, is a real no-no in my case. As if the blood tech didn't get enough, Dr. Woodman came in for three (3) more tubes; that totally wiped me out! He left saying he'd be right back. I tried to be slick by going down to the lounge. But I got so weak Mom and Bobby had to bring me back to my room in a wheelchair. Bobby read the 27th and the 23rd Psalms to me and gave me a beautiful plaque. It truly brightened my day and gave me more strength to go on.

When we returned, Dr. Woodman was back with the authorization papers for the surgery. I don't know why I felt so compelled to escape him; I guess I was afraid he wanted more blood. (smile) Anyway, I signed the papers; he left, and I took a nap. An hour later, transportation arrived to take me across the street to the main building to x-ray, and to go to the Hematology Department to check my 'clotting time'.

When I returned, the IV team was waiting with more needles and so was dinner. I was starved, weak, tired, and bombarded. Of course, dinner was cold—again! Bobby was here to visit again. The nurse wanted vital signs. Mom accidentally spilled soda on the bed; the nurse was upset because she had to change the linen, and dinner was still getting cold.

Nevertheless, I made it through the day; all of that is over now, and I can call it a night.

God manifested His power and Spirit many times over today. He constantly does little things to make me comfortable during these trying situations. God is still good and still blessing me in spite of it all. We thank Him.

Love, Susan

P. S. Bless Mom for not letting this day go unrecorded here on earth. Good Night. xxxxooxooxxoxo

April 1, 1983

Today they did the kidney biopsy. The doctors said the procedure was a success; no complications 'so far'. God has bought me through again, I thank Him. The surgery was a real trip! They didn't even put me to sleep! I was 'sedated' with Demerol (quite a nice high) but they couldn't put me completely 'under' with anesthesia because the kidney is a 'floating' organ and I had to breath a certain way during the surgery to move it away from my rib cage—it was wild, to say the least! You never know what you can endure until it's thrown at you, then *waa-laa*, inside you find the strength you need and you do it! Thank God for the strength.

This entry compliments of Mom also—May God richly bless her.

April 2, 1983

Well, I'm not really sure whether today was better than yesterday or not. Thank God I can write tonight, although it's still a little difficult. I thank God I can move. It was really a challenge to lay flat on my back without moving for a solid 24 hours after the surgery. I'm glad that's over.

They took the IV out this morning around ?—before dawn (as usual). And the surgery gave lupus center-stage. Although it was necessary to check out the condition of my kidneys, I'm now suffering with weakness like you wouldn't believe, or maybe by now, you would believe.

Anyway, Mom had to wash me up this morning. We started washing with me sitting in a chair in the bathroom, I couldn't stand more than for a few seconds at a time, so we tried the chair, but even that was too much and I was forced to lay back down before she could finish. She had to do the lower part of my body with me back in the bed.

Dr. Woodman and Dr. Dean came by this morning before leaving for the weekend. They seem to think the extreme weakness, dizziness, and nausea is probably due to lupus so they added another 20 mg. of steroids; "Only for today," they said. It seems to have done the trick; I feel considerably better now.

On the other hand, my surprise company today may have had something to do with how I feel too. They say "laughter is the best medicine," and that I did have. Lisa and Chaleese came by to visit today. They traveled three (3) hours on the bus just to see me! Definitely true friendship in every sense of the word! They came bearing tidings of great joy and gifts of love; beautiful tulips (tomorrow's Easter and I just *love* tulips! They had cards, a special little nightlight, and of course, an elephant, oo-oo-oop! The funny part though was teaching them how to help me get in and out of the bed. It was a trip! We even had an accident and spilled water in the bed (the third accident this weekend—I know the nurses are tired of me). (smile)

Generally speaking, the nurses have been the absolute pits (I just had to call four times for a pain pill). They rarely come in to check to see how I'm doing, then when they do, they seem to not really be concerned about doing their job too well, kinda like just going through the motions. The nice front with the birthday song sure did wear off fast. But experience has shown me that nurses are just people, too; sometimes you run across 'good' ones, sometimes 'not so good ones'. I just didn't 'luck out' this time so I thank God even more for Mom and friends like Lisa and Chaleese who care enough to help make my cross a little easier to bear. I was also glad to see them relieve Mom for a while, even if for just a little while.

I'm really upset with the nurses right about now, May God please forgive me. Praise His name for the resurrection of Jesus Christ so that forgiveness is possible.

Happy Easter!!!

April 3, 1983

Happy Easter! A.M.—Morning

Praise the Lord, Lord of Lord, King of Kings. God is so very good! Good does not adequately describe Him. The only word worthy to attribute to Him, the Holy One, is—HALLELUJAH!!!

Here in this hospital room all alone in my tears, He stopped by today to renew my strength once again. He's answering my every prayer. He even gave me a message, too, through the TV program I watched this morning. I can't do it justice on paper, but my heart and my mind understood. I prayed for Mom and I to have more strength and love between us, so last night He led her to take the initiative to read the Word to us and study the crucifixion of Christ. It gave us both more strength, wisdom, and understanding of our situation.

Another thing He has done is taken away the sad, discouraged, and isolated feeling I had about my situation and my limitations. God not only is changing the situation but He also showed me the purposes for the situation. It seemed negative at first glance, but it really did have a purpose and positive results in the end. He continues to show me more of His power and His love. I praise His name for that and so much more. He works so diligently and does so much more than I can see. He seems to always be on His J-O-B of being G-O-D.

I thank God for being GOD and I thank God for sending Christ to the earth. And I thank Christ for coming to earth and dying for me, but most of all, I thank Christ for rising again!!! Happy Easter!

P.M.—Evening

More blessings! I just don't know how to thank God. I'm so unworthy, especially when I think back to what a bad (sinful) person I used to be in the past, and now I'm receiving so many blessings in so many ways. I was blind but now I see—I thank God for the vision.

I now have an inner peace that passes all understanding just like the Word says I can have. That just goes to show that His Word is truth and it stands. I am His child and His love surpasses all! Christ still lives and that's what Easter is all about—my spirit is so high right now—words just don't suffice, so I'll just say thank God for all of His goodness . . . G-Nite

April 4, 1983

Today was better than yesterday, physically. I knew it would be. The nurses turned me on to a new kind of wheelchair since I'm having problems walking and standing for long periods of time. I could shower in it while still sitting down—what a trip, huh? It was kind'a strange. In my mind I kept thinking I shouldn't have been getting it wet.

Afterwards, she helped me grease down. I'm so tired of always having to go to such great lengths to take care of my skin. We've tried every cortisone cream on the market, none of which really help, even at $18 a tube. So now Mom and the nurses are wrapping my body mummy-fashion in plastic wrap to aid the creams to soak into my skin better. The dermatologists think it might help. One ointment for my face and another for the rest of my body, and still open lesions from head to toe, literally. Oh, how I look forward to the day when I can just use lotion like ordinary people. Right now I'm as desperate as the doctors are to find something that will work. Having to wear plastic gloves to shower or even get dressed is going a bit far, but I'll just have to deal until my change comes because I know I can't stand anything to touch my raw hands. Anyway, Mom was able to sleep a little later this morning since the nurse helped me wash up.

More beautiful cards and calls. Thank God for that. And another miracle!

The doctors informed me today that they were forced to do the biopsy a little different than normal due to my severe case of scoliosis. They said they had to go in the right side of my back and perform the procedure three (3) centimeters from my liver. They said it was "remarkable" not to see even a trace of blood in my urine. Not even a trace!! They say it's remarkable—I say it's GOD!

All of this is a miracle! The fact that I'm even going through this is a miracle! The fact that I'm still here on this earth today is a miracle! I say 'miracle' because all of these things are 'humanly impossible'. I've been so sick in the past, I know it was only God who carried me, just like the poem "Footprints" says. And even with the surgery just a few days ago, I know it was only God who carried me through that too; there is no way I could have borne that kind of pain nor experience on my own or in my own strength. Praise the name of the Lord. The test results from the biopsy haven't come back yet, but I know God still has that under control too.

I met another lupus patient across the hall tonight. I'm still kind of weak, so I'll have to talk with her more later.

The guy at the other end of the hall is leaving for Fishers tomorrow for paralysis therapy. I pray God will give him and his family all the power, strength, and courage they need to deal with what lies ahead. He's only 19 yrs. old. He was in a motorcycle accident and now he's paralyzed from the neck down. Things like that let you know how bad things could really be. God bless everyone . . .

G-Nite

April 5, 1983

Today was a little better, but just a little! 6:00–8:00 A.M. this morning was OK. I awoke and meditated, but after breakfast it was back to bed. I ate good, but by the time Dr. Dean, Dr. Little, and Dr. Green came by at 8:30 A.M., I was extremely fatigued, weak, and nauseous.

Nevertheless, this evening was considerably better. I was suppose to write more but I called Jenny tonight and we talked for about three (3) hours. Although I thoroughly enjoyed it and it was very much needed, it really tired me out. I also just took a sleeping pill because it's so difficult to fall asleep on such high dosages of steroids. So I'm beginning to drift off now . . . My God is so good—I thank Him so! Praise the name of the Lord!

Susan

Well, today was pretty laid back. This morning 6:00–8:00 A.M. was pretty good again, but my energy dwindled drastically after breakfast. Maybe they're putting something in the food. (smile) They increased my steroid dosage from 30 mg to 40 mg again and gave them all to me at 8:00 this morning instead of in two separate doses, so the overall day was a little better. (Steroids take about three hours to actually 'kick in' before the full effect is felt and the 'boost' from one dose usually lasts about twelve hours).

Today was OK. God blessed me to be able to stand while taking a shower; of course, this was after the student nurse rode me down the hall to the bathroom in the wheelchair; can't do everything—yet! Still, I could at least stand long enough to shower once there.

We were required to watch a film today on hypertension. I was able to walk across the hall, even if the movie was boring. I had an accident sitting down in the chair too hard and stretched a muscle or something; the resulting discomfort has been present all evening. The kidney specialists checked it out and said everything looked alright. No damage done. Thank God for protection.

Anyway, it was quite a scare. I thought I had injured the incision. I must be careful from now on so I don't disturb the blood clots that have formed around the biopsy spot, so the doctor says. They're still checking for the appearance of blood in my urine. Can't they accept a miracle when they see one—obviously not. Poor things!

I talked to Aunt Evelyn this morning and Aunt Shirley tonight. It was so very nice to hear their voices laced with love and concern. I truly thank God for them, their love, and their support. I can't imagine how it would have been over the years going through all of this without them. Tim called tonight also. It was very thoughtful of him since he just lost his father recently. I know he's going through a rough time right now, a true friend to take the time to encourage me.

I was confronted with a new problem tonight—mental confusion and disorientation. It really tripped me out! It was incredibly frightening not having proper use of my mental faculties. It was too bizarre for me to even try to explain. My thoughts didn't properly connect and my sentences made no sense. Part of me could understand that I was a little off, but another part of me kept trying to communicate haphazard, disjointed, mixed up make believes. Truly it was scary! It was more of a trip than anything I have ever experienced, and I've experienced quite a bit during this short lifetime. Neither I nor the doctors knew if this strange reaction was attributed to the disease or the medication. All I know is I am so glad it passed. God is so good; I love Him so.

P. S. I received a get well card from one of the kids in the Youth Fellowship Program at my church today. Fruits of my labor—my living is not in vain. Thank God for the reinforcement and encouragement.

G-Nite!

April 7, 1983

Dear Lord, thank you! The doctors came by with the biopsy results; my kidneys are not damaged as bad as they thought. I do have focal renal involvement which is the least life-threatening of all possible kinds, I'm told. The bad news is that this makes the decisions of treatment a lot more difficult; the doctors aren't quite sure what direction to take now. They feel Cytoxin is a 'good' choice, but it can cause sterility. I'm too young for that and have no kids yet. On the other hand, the high dose of steroids in addition to plaquinell and other anti-malarial drugs would be a 'good' choice and possibly successful in treating my case, but they have other bad side effects. The doctors want me to make the decision! Who am I to make such a decision? I don't know!!! I don't know anything! I've done all the research possible on these drugs and I still don't have the 'right' answer. Mom and I went to the chapel this evening; we meditated, prayed, and left it in the Lord's hands. He knows a lot more than we do—especially about what the future holds. He knows what's best.

Bobby and his wife came by tonight and what a blessing they were. Mom and I had already prayed for an answer to our situation and believed in our hearts that God would manifest Himself. The Word of the Lord says if we believe in our hearts, not doubting then those things which we say shall come to pass. (St. Mark 11:23) We already believed in our hearts and the conversation with Bob and Sylva provided us with the opportunity to confess our faith with our mouths. God is so good and I know He's directing my path. We had to line up with the Word to make the Word work for us and God made that possible.

God also manifested Himself through another miracle today—the Fredericks. This woman just wandered into my room from out of nowhere and started telling us this story about her husband who had been asleep for days. The doctors had given him too much anesthesia during a surgical procedure. The entire hospital staff was frantic and feared a possible lawsuit. They had taken him to the ICU and were expecting him to die. She was full of tears and fear. It was obvious to me that God had sent this woman into my room to talk to us so we would pray for her. Deep down inside I knew God would protect her husband, and He did.

After our conversation with her, Mom and I went down to the chapel and prayed very earnestly for them, believing that God only wanted us to ask so He could do. As we were approaching the doorway to my room, we heard the phone ringing. It was Mrs. Frederick telling us that she didn't know exactly what had happened, but her husband had just woken up!!!! Maybe she didn't know what had happened, but we sure did—God had answered yet another prayer even before we could finish praying just like He says He would do in His Word. (Isaiah 65:24) Praise the name of the Lord!

Today's health was a little bit better, especially tonight, and my spirit and Mom's spirit is still being strengthened. All things truly do "work together for good to them that love the Lord and are called according to His purpose." (Romans 8:28)

April 8, 1983

Well, it's time to move on to the next step now. The doctors, all seven (7) of them, came by during the course of this day to finalize their findings and determine the final course of treatment. Results—the kidney biopsy was a real success. The tissue specimen was good and the lab tests went well. The tests showed I have focal proliferative membranous renal involvement—meaning I have two types of kidney disease—but both moderate and standing at the present time. Thank God! The kidneys aren't as bad as they thought they were, so they decided against using Cytoxin for right now. This was a prayer answered, too, because I had asked God to lead them and me to make the 'best' decision, seeing that He and He alone knows what my future holds. He knows about the side-effects and the long-lasting effects of such treatment. And *waalaa*, He worked it out! Praise Him—again!

The biopsy caused a double flare-up of lupus so they want to keep me at 45 mg/day of steroids for another month, 40 mg/day for the second month, and then a return visit to see the doctor.

One may ask how I can praise the Lord in the midst of such a terrible storm in my life; well, I praise Him for the shelter and the peace in the midst of the storm. Each time the blustery winds blow, I'm protected. I also thank Him for closing the windows when the forceful rain comes. It's the little things that mean so much. The storm in my life is here; there isn't anything I can do about that, but I can seek protection while it lasts.

Dr. Woodman put everything into proper perspective by explaining the purpose of the high dosage of prednisone. He said if it's sustained long enough, it will cause my body to build up enough resistance to disease activity, thus preventing flare-ups in the future and hastening a quicker remission. I've felt that 1984 was going to be my year. God has even spoken to my spirit that "My time has come," so maybe this is it?? Whatever the outcome, I still know who holds the key!

Mom and I just came back up from the chapel. We took our problems there and only felt it right to take our thanksgiving there, too. Praise the Lord!

The understanding and knowledge we received from the medical profession here is very impressive. I've learned so much more about the treatment of lupus. I have a newfound respect for Dr. Sykes and his judgement which will definitely help in the long run with my treatments at home.

Bobby came by with more flowers today. And some new people I met yesterday gave me a little stuffed animal and a card. They said I had a beautiful spirit. I really needed that reinforcement. Especially now that I'm puffy from the higher dosage of medicine in addition to my skin being so broken out. It's good that something is beautiful about me. (smile) God is so good, keeping me on the 'right' track—looking at the spiritual realm instead of the physical realm. He just taught me from a number of books in the New Testament including James chapter 4 and chapter 5. God also ministered to me from the book of Daniel and about 'patience'. Patience is one of the main things I need right now and that's what I've been praying for lately. But it's still kind of hard to grasp, so He gave me my 'daily bread' to meditate and feast upon. "To whom much is given, much is required" (St Luke 12:48b) and God has given me a lot. However, I know He will supply all that's necessary for me to do His will no matter how difficult the task may seem. Because it's His show, His purpose; I am His child and everything on earth belongs to Him!!! (Psalms 24:1)

Love and praises to my God Jehovah,
G-Nite

April 9, 1983

Well, the day is done again and, boy, was it full of surprises. Dr. Forester took one look at me this morning and said I couldn't leave until at least Monday. She said the other symptoms are too active. So Mom and I called Uncle Bora to cancel our plans to go home. Mom said she wasn't too disappointed but she had nervous energy today, so I tend to think otherwise. Anyway, we all have to bear our own cross and I guess that's hers, the uncertainties of tomorrow. I'm just sorry it's through me or maybe I should be happy that I'm the channel God is using to teach her His way!

I was really depressed and a little down a minute ago. I had an urge to walk down the hall. I wandered into Rose's room and talked to her for a while. She really helped me put things into a better perspective, she was born not able to walk and still hasn't to this day. Her words of encouragement were, "Don't give up!" She says, when she's feeling down, she concentrates on the things she can do and not on what she can't do, always looking at the good instead of the bad.

Another patient walked in with more words of wisdom and encouragement as she stated that, "Life is full of give and take;

we must be more willing to give instead of always so eager to take from life." I listened to what these two people had to say because they've been dealing a lot longer that I have—they must have learned something. God is so good to open my eyes tonight. I was temporarily blinded by darkness and despair. Jesus Christ is the light of the world. He lives in others and He lives in me. Thank God. Nitey-Nite.

April 10, 1983

Depression and discontentment of having/living with lupus subsides because "This sickness is not unto death, but for the glory of God, that the Son of God might be glorified by it." (St. John 11:4) This is the Word that the Lord quickened in my spirit tonight. It's incredible—I can say that I know this to be true in my life, with me. I can't say *how* I know; I just do!

April 11, 1983

A.M.—It looks as if I'm finally turning the corner. It's 7:00 A.M. and I've already washed my face, brushed my teeth, and meditated. I think I'll be leaving Wednesday, but I'm still taking it one day and sometimes one hour at a time. I don't even know what today holds or how I'll feel after breakfast, but my spirit is calm right now so I'll be OK.

P.M.—Today was OK; I was right. Breakfast was followed by a downswing, but I did finally muster up enough strength to take a shower. The nurses let Mom take me outside for some fresh air. It was very welcomed and much needed after so many days of being cooped up. There was a cute little courtyard with some benches where we sat. Then we walked a little, a very little. (smile) The biopsy spot started hurting so I was ready to 'chill out'. In no time at all, the arthritis and weakness started up—what a bummer!

Dr. Forester said to wait til tomorrow and see how things are, referring to when I can go home. I guess this is how I'll learn patience; these experiences give a whole new meaning to the word *uncertainty*. I don't have a problem with her advice cause I don't want to be worse when I get home. I don't mind staying here until I get strong enough to make the trip, but still patience must play her part in the wait. "Let patience have her perfect work." (James 1:4)

I ended up witnessing to some ladies down the hall tonight. I gave one lady with a nervous condition, the serenity prayer. She had never even seen it before. It seemed to be exactly what she needed. She has a problem worrying. With God, there's no need to do that.

I hadn't planned any of this. I just followed my spirit and God's lead to check on the other lady in her room who had just undergone a heart catherization. I thought the Lord sent me in to her, but instead He used me to minister to both of them. Before I knew it, the Holy Spirit filtered through me directly to them. Praise God !!! G-Nite.

A few days later, we left the *Freak Zoo*, as I so fondly named it because of the bizarre cases that seem to be so prevalent there. Doctors tend to send their most unique, unsolvable cases to learning institutions of that sort, and believe me, they were definitely unique.

I still thanked God for such a place where He shares such a wealth of information and knowledge with mankind. I left with a much better understanding of the strange illness that had so mysteriously taken over my life.

Overjoyed that the treatments had been so successful in curing the skin lesions and that I no longer had to be wrapped in plastic wrap, I was under the full assumption that I was on my way to better health. I was looking forward to recuperating with great expectations when, in less than a weeks time, I found myself back in the hospital. No, not Clarkston; that would have taken too much preparation. This was an emergency, and there wasn't much time. I had to be rushed to a local hospital closer to home. Yes, rushed—like in *immediately*. But not for the lesions that had caused so many problems only weeks before, nor for complications from the kidney biopsy that had been such a serious threat. I wasn't even being admitted for the disabling arthritis that sporadically traveled from finger joint to toe joint in a matter of minutes and occasionally locked every muscles in my body. Neither was the current problem any of the other fourteen so-called clinical symptoms that I so frequently found myself coping with; instead, it was something totally new. Variety is the spice of life, they say, so why not throw in a curveball to add some excitement and get me off kilter.

I guess that was the attitude of my fate, and a few days after my return home from Clarkston, I found myself burning with fever and too weak to get out of bed—not the flu-like weakness I was used to, but an incapacitating kind of weakness. It got so bad that Mom couldn't even wait until dawn, but in a frantic voice said, "I think we need to call Dr. Sykes, *now!*" It didn't matter that it was only four o'clock in the morning. After hearing a description of my condition, Dr. Sykes immediately commanded, "Bring her to the office now, and I'll meet you there."

The only response I had was complete relief. I felt as if I had been run over by a Mack truck. Between numerous episodes of vomiting and gagging, along with having to sit every few seconds for fear of fainting, Mom was able to get me dressed and to the doctor's office.

Upon arrival, the nurse met us at the curb with a well-trusted friend of a chair with two wheels. Once on the table, all I could do was mumble. With my weak voice, I begged, "Please make me feel better." And I meant that from the bottom of my heart. I really didn't care what Dr. Sykes did or what he was going to do, as long as he made me feel better.

Usually I detested medicines, especially steroids. The doctors would always have a fight on their hands trying to increase the dosage, not only because of the bad side-effects, but because it would take years of weaning just to reach a lower dose. But this time I didn't care. This time my brain registered a big fat zero in analyzing my problem or my desire for treatment. The only thing that registered in my overheated brain at the time was how unbearably ill I was and how I needed some help. Usually, I would try to assist the doctors with treatment—looking at the alternatives, checking out the pros and cons of the situation, looking at future consequences, but not this time. This time I didn't care. This time none of that mattered.

It didn't even matter that I would look like a blimp the entire time I would be undergoing treatment. Nothing at all mattered except the fact that I desperately needed some relief from my discomfort. No rational thinking was going on here, only a gut reaction to a physical problem that seemed out of control.

Lying on my back on the hard, narrow, black leather table in his office that morning, I had only two concerns: that I would soon feel better and that someone would give me something cold to drink. As the fever ravaged my body, my entire insides felt like a desert. The feeling better part would probably take some time, I thought, but water was available right there at hand!

After a brief examination, Dr. Sykes left the room. In the same feeble mumble, I asked the nurse, who had been assigned to stay by my side, for some water. With neither the strength nor energy for a complete sentence, I simply tried to get the point across. "Waaa-terr," I requested.

Giving me her undivided attention, she compassionately stated, "I can't give you any water, but I can give you a little ice." That sounded even better; it was colder. I nodded slightly, relieved to get anything cold.

I lay there a little puzzled at exactly what was going on. I had been ill for years, but this, no doubt, was a new twist. I kept trying to ignore the message I had received just before leaving home as Mom called the doctor. Each time it would surface, I would subconsciously push it further and further out of my mind—not because I didn't believe my God, but because it was almost unbelievable to me that He would speak to me in such an exact fashion, revealing the truth so prophetically to me. I *knew* I had felt the Spirit of God unction my spirit, telling me that I had pneumonia. I don't know how to explain it except to say that I knew it was God speaking to my spirit. You know when we say, *I knew something was telling me that?* Well, I knew my something was God. His voice was very familiar, but this way was new to me. I was used to God speaking to me, but nothing so clear or precise as this had ever happened to me before. I kept telling myself that it was just me trying to diagnose my own case, but deep down inside I knew that was not it at all. From where would I get the idea of pneumonia? I knew nothing at all about the illness. I had never known anyone that had it, and I had never read anything at all about it. I didn't even know what it was like to have it. Although, all of this was true, I still kept trying to talk myself out of this message coming from my God, for that was a little too far out for even me. But I knew that it had, in fact, come from Him.

My attention was quickly returned to instant gratification as the nurse put one of the little pieces of frozen water on my lips. I felt the first sense of relief I had experienced in hours, as it slid into my mouth and melted on contact. "More! More," I begged, pleading for more relief. She complied with my wishes for a few more pieces, then stated in a motherly yet very professional tone, "That's enough for now; we don't want you to start regurgitating again." Too weak to argue, I just appeased myself by trying to remember the cool sensation I had just felt.

In no time at all, Dr. Sykes reentered the room. With a much too serious look plastered on his slender pale face, he stated, "I'm sending you to the hospital straight from here. Your mother and I have made all the arrangements."

I had been so preoccupied with my refreshing friend, the ice, that I hadn't even missed Mom's presence. *Strange,* I thought to myself, *they usually at least let me go home and get some things first.* But even that didn't seem important, as I responded with my same question in the same feeble voice, "Can you make me feel better?"

He looked with compassion in his eyes and answered, "After we're sure what's going on. I think you have pneumonia, but we have to be certain."

My spirit-man quickened on the inside of me in response to his words, like activity in a pregnant mother's womb. God was right!

Mom felt I needed her undivided attention at this point, so she opted to call my Uncle Bora to drive us the other fifteen miles to the hospital. Only too willing to help, he arrived at Dr. Sykes' office in no time at all. I don't know how I got in the car, but I soon realized we were on our way.

With Mom and I in the back seat, the ride seemed endless. I would drift out, then back again, only to find us still riding and me still feeling terrible. It didn't seem as if I would go to sleep, but I would go someplace else. It was as if I was maybe in and out of consciousness—I probably was. I would just come back and find myself in another phase of transport. Back to earth again I came, finding us at the emergency entrance of the hospital. We had finally arrived.

Uncle Bora went in to get a wheelchair, and instead of me waiting there with Mom, I went off again into never-never land. Back to earth I came, as Mom, Bora, and the accompanying nurse got me into the wheelchair. I tried diligently to assist them as much as I could, which really wasn't any assistance at all; my equilibrium was shot, my body was weak, and the rest of me seemed to be out to lunch. I heard the nurse's voice way off in a distance, almost like through a tunnel, or from another planet, as she explained, "Dr. Sykes' office called and made all the necessary arrangements, so we can just take her straight to her room." Nodding to Mom, she added, "You can come down to admittance later and give them any additional information they may need."

Good, I thought, *finally a bed. I can lie down.* Then rationale kicked in, and I realized I must have been pretty sick for them to let me pass all the red tape and procedures! Fear suddenly gripped me. This was for real! What in the world was going on? I'd come close to death many times before, but I'd never felt this bad. This time I really felt like I could actually be dying! And the steps taken by the doctor were so drastic. Was this it? Was I really gonna check out of here this time?

The most frightening part of it all was the fact that I couldn't account for the periods when I seemed to just take a break from it all and disappear. What was happening to me? Where did I go? I couldn't just cease to be; or could I? All of these questions bombarded my mind as I tried desperately to search for answers.

My attention swiftly drifted from those thoughts, and I was cognizant of the fact that I was in my other reality; the one where I could see, hear, and touch, as I rode to the room and they undressed me for bed. The nurse was talking to Mom about the orders Dr. Sykes had phoned in. I heard her voice again fade into the distance and nothing at all registered, almost as if it's first in a foreign language; then it faded completely out into nothingness. *Here I go again*, I said to myself, but I couldn't stick around if I wanted to.

I'm not sure how long I was gone that time, but I was bought back by more nurses with a laundry list of instructions: catheterizations, blood withdrawals, lab work, and of course, x-rays. I was accustomed to all of this, for I had been through these kinds of tests many times before. The difference this time, though, was that they all came to me, instead of me going to them. Usually, I would trample down various hallways to the lab or to radiology, but not this time. This time they all came to me—even the huge monstrous x-ray machine had to pay *me* a visit. I probably would have been impressed and felt very important had not the 104-degree temperature diverted my every attention.

A few hours later, in walked Dr. Sykes with a grave look of despair upon his face. Dr. Sykes was a calm, mild-mannered gentleman. Things had to be pretty bad to spark a look like that from him. He stood at my bedside for a brief moment, looking down upon me, almost as if in disbelief. He had seen me sick before, but never quite this bad. He stood quietly, as if trying to search for the right words to say. I couldn't focus on anything too long, but with much concentration, I was able to focus on him long enough to see the devastated look on his face before my eyes closed again. I heard him ask my mom how I was doing and add that the diagnosis was one of walking pneumonia, as if I didn't already know. The Lord had been one up on us, and it had taken us this long just to catch up.

Although I didn't say a word, my initial response was that of despair also. I felt as if I already had enough to deal with. I felt as if I really didn't need nor could I handle anything else. Nevertheless, God was in control—and I soon discovered that He had a purpose in mind and a plan in action. I also found that this particular episode was only a forerunner used to set the stage for a more important and most unique life-changing experience.

My fluctuating existence here and there, drifting in and out, continued on. Exactly how long, I'm not quite sure. Being semiconscious for days, in and out of what we know as reality, I laid there slowly losing my will to fight. I couldn't really understand it, but after a while, it just didn't seem worthwhile to fight anymore, not that I made a conscious decision to feel that way. It's just that I wasn't spending much time *here* anymore. Here just didn't seem important. I wasn't a part of this world, and it just didn't seem to be where I was supposed to be. I no longer felt as if this was my home. I seemed to be spending the majority of my time someplace else, perhaps in another dimension.

Another dimension—in another place, a place that seemed so very peaceful and pleasant, incomprehensibly peaceful and pleasant. Here I had to fight; there I didn't! There I felt nothing at all but sheer comfort. Why struggle when there's an alternative, especially when the alternative feels so very right? I was at peace during those out to lunch lapses, but each time I returned to what was transpiring here in this physical realm, I was faced with chaos, pain, and ultimate discomfort. Which would you choose?

I received three different antibiotics intravenously around the clock for five consecutive days, with no change at all in my physical condition. It seemed as if all efforts were futile. The 104-degree temperature would attempt to break, only to shoot back up again. So, in a desperate attempt to save my life, the doctor decided to run one more test. The technicians lowered a long tube down my throat into my chest cavity to withdraw some of the fluid that seemed to be just sitting in my lungs. It was their hope that, in analyzing this mucous, they might be able to identify an antibiotic to which the bacteria would respond positively. Although I could tell the test was a little uncomfortable, I was too sick to really pay close attention to what was going on. However, I do remember feeling relieved that it was over. Even then, God had a way of protecting me from the pain.

Talking during that time was very difficult for me. I couldn't formulate thoughts or sentences in my brain, nor did I have the strength to speak. I tried to pray, silently, but had no success with that either. I even attempted to recite the twenty-third Psalm in my mind and failed. I said, "The Lord is my shepherd," and my mind went completely blank. I couldn't remember one word of the rest of the declaration! A declaration that had been so deeply engraved in my heart and mind since childhood had simply vanished from my recollection. I once heard that the prayers of God's people are stored in heaven. I hoped that was the case with me because I really did need some help.

The hospital receptionist held a card with my room number on it, but it also stated *No visitors*. My family waited patiently for the minister to arrive.

While lying flat on my back in that bed, looking like Frankenstein's daughter with IV tubes alternating between both arms, hands, and even my feet at times, and oxygen tubes up both nostrils, I opened my eyes. To my astonishment, I saw *myself* come into the room—the room in which I thought I was already lying. There I was coming through the glass window pane that wasn't even open. I saw me! I saw myself dressed in the same blue and white hospital gown, minus the many tubes, and a head full of hair like that I possessed before any of this craziness with lupus ever started. I looked as though I was floating, drifting forward towards myself on the bed. In a split second, I was gone. I simply disappeared, but the second lasted long enough for my brain to register what my eyes had seen.

Although I was astonished, I was not afraid. The strange thing about these spiritual experiences is that I was *never* frightened. I can't speak for others, but I can say that the ones I experienced with my Creator were wonderful. During the time that the actual experience was occurring, I was on a completely different plane of existence—totally in the spiritual realm. This was easy and simple, since the essence of all human beings is spiritual. When having an out of body experience, the spirit soars without limitation. There are no restrictions etched by thoughts derived from our five senses. Because the force that created me is a spirit, it is only possible to communicate with Him by and with my spirit. Strangely enough, when I communicated with Him on His level, there was no fear, only peace and love.

Soon the minister arrived. Surprisingly enough, as we prepared to pray, the Holy Spirit, God's Spirit, urged my spirit to lead the prayer. It was not an ordinary urge at all, but one so strong that it totally consumed me to the point of complete obedience. I could not ignore it, nor could I refuse it; all I could do was obey it. My rational mind was intact for a brief moment, and it questioned my behavior. *You can't pray*, it confronted me; *how can you pray when you're barely able to talk? You couldn't even recite the twenty-third Psalm, and those words were already there for you! How can you pray? You take these sporadic lunch breaks, and you aren't even here most of the time. And if by chance you could get the words together, your voice is too weak for the others to hear you.* This whole train of thought amazed me; I hadn't been able to think that much, that clearly, nor that rationally in days. What was really going on here? The conversation continued, but the words and their logic just seemed to roll over my head like water off a duck's back. None of that mattered. The only thing that mattered was that I *had* to do it! My spirit had made complete connection with my Creator's Spirit, and I had neither choice nor control. I had no say-so at all in the matter.

My Mom, my Aunt Evelyn, the minister and I all joined hands; I proceeded to speak, and God's Holy Spirit just took over. In no time at all I began to speak with a new sense of authority. Physical strength came from nowhere. I began to speak loudly and powerfully, and perspiration commenced to cover my entire body. As I prayed, it was as if no one else was in the room except me and my God. It seemed as if He directed my every word. His Spirit told my spirit exactly what to pray back to His Spirit. It was really weird! Then again, most spiritual matters are to the human mind. God's Word says that His thoughts are not our thoughts and that His ways are not our ways. The carnal mind is contrary to God; spiritual matters are foolish to the carnal—natural—mind. So that explained why it seemed so weird to me.

By the time we had finished, both my gown and the bed were drenched, and the nurse had to change us both. Before I knew it, my fever had begun to break. My temperature continued to decrease with each reading. The next morning it was down to one hundred degrees. As time progressed, they discontinued intravenous feedings of the antibiotics—first one, then another, then another. Within a few days, I was taking all necessary antibiotics by mouth instead of IV and was able to talk.

Needless to say, my family, the doctor, and I were all overjoyed at this new change in my condition. We all gave the credit and glory to God because we knew we had seen no change until the prayer. That particular minister has since gone home to be with the Lord, but he praised God for witnessing that miracle until his dying day!

That was my introduction to the great power of the Holy Spirit. You see, I really *did* see my spirit come back into the room that day. I believe it went to the Lord to receive special power, God's special healing power, God's anointing. The Word of God says it's the anointing of God that destroys the yoke. No doubt, I was in the yoke of bondage to that fever, and it took the anointing of God to destroy it. You see, everything that we can see, hear, smell, taste, and touch here in the physical realm, including illness, is only a manifestation of a greater reality that exists first in the spiritual realm. So if the spiritual realm is the basis of all reality, then all battles can best fought in that realm, also. However, fighting is only one aspect of the issue—what about winning?

The key to winning is to fight with the most powerful tool or force available. Since God is the author of all creation, then it reasons to say, that He also is the main source of all things; He is all power. If He is all power, then He is the most powerful force, and in Him lies the most powerful tool. Since God is a spirit, then it only reasons to say that in His Spirit lies the power, the source, and the tool to win the battle. So when fighting, whether naturally or spiritually, since we now know that they are both one in the same, if we go to the source of all power to get our power, then there is no way we can lose; we can only win!

He's the Commanding Executive Officer of the universe. He's the man in charge—the Main Man. His Spirit, better known as the Holy Spirit, endowed me with what I needed to win. He knew He had given me what I needed to effectively fight my battle and win—and that is why I was led to say the prayer, instead of the minister. You see, God uses ordinary people more that we realize.

I don't have the answer as to why He chose to bless me with that power instead of the minister, but He did; and when I began to pray and use it, allowing it to flow, it worked!

Recuperating from the ordeal was another hurdle, but God doesn't do anything halfway; that was just the beginning of my healing. The next few days were plagued with excessive diarrhea, nothing but bedpan activity. I still wasn't strong enough to get out of bed, so the bedpan became my necessary companion. Needing it almost every hour on the hour was strange because I hadn't eaten in weeks. Nevertheless, I later understood that, in order for my healing to manifest completely, God had to cleanse my body of all the residual bacteria, infection, and chemicals from the medicines. Hallelujah! The doctors didn't understand, so they tested samples of my stool, thinking something was wrong. I knew everything was alright, but they had to see for themselves.

Days passed, and soon the cleansing process was complete. It was then time to start eating to regain some of the strength I had lost. This led to a new and different kind of struggle.

Taking pills by mouth had been extremely painful, but I thought my throat was just sore from all the tubes. I was ready for a meal! My stomach was finally hungry, and I thought this was my big day to eat something. They were actually going to let me out of bed to sit in a chair for a while and try some food. *How exciting*, I thought. But much to my surprise—and nothing should have surprised me at this point—things were nothing like I expected.

Once standing, I realized how weak I really was. With one hand reaching for Mom, my Rock of Gibraltar, and the other hand on the bedrail, my legs quickly sent distress signals to my brain. My leg muscles told my brain that they felt like putty and there was no way they could support the rest of my body. *You'd better sit back down*, it warned me, as it processed this new information and offered a solution. I flopped back down on the side of the bed. "Wow! . . . Coming back from the dead is hard work," I jokingly told my Mom. Our smiles danced together once again. A little humor never hurts. Sometimes we were forced to use it just to help lighten our serious load.

I looked down at my feet for the first time in weeks and was quickly reminded of the many health problems that had plagued my life before this most recent crisis with pneumonia.

The sight of my feet was only too familiar to me. Swelling usually accompanied any flareup of lupus, and this was no exception. The ever-persistent fluid retention from the higher dose of steroids and intravenous treatments had quadrupled during the past week, and my feet and ankles responded by swelling twice their normal size—so much so that when I did finally walk, I could feel the fluid swishing around beneath my skin. *I sure am glad they can't withdraw fluid from the feet, like they can from the knees*, I thought. I'd had that done before, and I knew how painful it was. I smiled to myself, aware that I had avoided at least one more needle.

The fluid retention wasn't just a problem for me because it made me look bad. Looks are only superficial. I was more concerned with the principle of the matter. My body was not designed to carry the forced excessive weight gain of the steroids, sometimes as much as sixty pounds, depending on the dosage. God simply did not design me that way. I was small-framed; I was not born overweight, and I was not an overeater. Carrying that much weight around just wasn't natural or normal for me. It was a condition placed on me unwillingly by synthetic means, and that was what really disturbed me.

Nevertheless, I had dealt with this many times before, and I knew there would be plenty of time to work with it, so I just pushed it to the back of my mind for the time being.

I immediately transferred my attention to the tray of food across the room. Noticing the focus of my eyes and still ready to help in any way she could, Mom said, "Would you like me to pull it over to you?"

"No," I replied; "I want to go over to it." The same gusto to overcome, as the old Susan, emerged. I contemplated briefly, as thoughts of the previous days' experiences flashed through my mind—but only briefly, for there was a much more pressing issue at hand: breakfast!

I struggled to stand. Every inch of my being felt as if it was truly the zombie that it was, finally being bought back to life. *Only a few more steps to the chair*, I encouraged myself. Finally, I made it! The sense of accomplishment I felt was incredible. I hadn't walked in weeks.

"Mmmmm!" Mom expressed, as she removed the brown plastic cover from the plate. "This looks pretty good. What do you want to try first?"

My actions spoke for me, as I reached for the little packet of jelly. I didn't have enough energy to act and talk at the same time, so I let my actions speak for me. She quickly responded by joining me in my efforts, as she prepared my toast with butter and jam, while I simultaneously reached for the silverware. Surprisingly, I noticed that much of the tenderness from the skin lesions on my hands that had been so very painful just weeks ago in Clarkston had disappeared. "I guess the higher dose of steroids did some good after all," I remarked sarcastically. Mom's eyes left the toast and raised to my face in search of what I was referring to. "Look, my hands," I stated, and we shared another smile, excited about any improvement at all. Wearing gloves to protect my hands from utensils and any other hard object, whether sharp or blunt, seemed to be a thing of the past, and we were very glad.

"Let's just skip the cereal and go for the food," I exclaimed. "My stomach is screaming." The juice burned like acid on an open wound. I couldn't handle it. *OK, we won't try that*, I said to myself, thinking it's just too soon to try something so strong, but I had the same problem with the eggs and couldn't even chew the toast. "What's wrong with me," I asked, searching Mom's face with a questioning look. "I can't eat anything! Call the nurse," I screamed as anxiety mounted.

Determined as usual, I continued trying to eat something on the tray, anything on the tray, while we waited for the nurse to respond to our call, but still the results was the same—burning, aching, tormenting pain. Finally the nurse arrived.

She was just as puzzled as we were, yet she tried to console me by saying, "Well, just try to drink your juice, and I'll notify your doctor when he arrives."

"When he arrives?" I repeat. "When will that be? I'm starving!"

"He's due any minute now," she stated reassuringly.

"OK, I'll wait," I agreed reluctantly, as if I really had a choice. But no juice, that hurt worst than the food! So Mom and I made our way back to the bed to wait for Dr. Sykes.

Shortly thereafter, Dr. Sykes arrived. His examination of my mouth and throat yielded a very disheartening conclusion. The antibiotics, in their attempt to kill the bacteria of the pneumonia, had inadvertently burned my mouth, throat, esophagus and stomach lining in the process, leaving behind a sea of open ulcers. So, now I not only had to contend with the open ulcers from the skin lacerations over ninety percent of my body, but now internal lesions as well. What a trip! So how was I suppose to eat when even plain water burned so profusely?

It took a while and a lot of hard work and perseverance, but I made it through that ordeal. Although very slowly, things did eventually get better. Dr. Sykes ordered a bland diet and liquid Xylocaine for me to keep at my bedside. I would spread it on every part of my mouth, swish it around, and swallow before each meal and many times throughout the day, just to make the pain bearable. I was able to eat enough to kill the hunger pangs, but never enough to get full. Praying each and every step of the way, God supplied me with the strength to successfully get through. There was no cure for this problem I had—only time could heal my wounds. Only the natural healing process of my body inside and out would rid me of my discomforts.

Shortly after Mother's Day, I was released from the hospital, again. I returned home on a higher dose of steroids than before. That made little sense to me, since Dr. Sykes had stated that the pneumonia had been steroid-induced; talk about being between a rock and a hard place. How could I win? Nevertheless, I continued to trust Dr. Sykes judgement. It had proven to be somewhat beneficial in the past, and I really didn't see any other alternative. I started recuperating at home on a sixty milligrams per day regime of steroids, instead of the one hundred and eighty milligrams per day I had previously received intravenously in the hospital.

Days at home were slow, but nights were a lot worse. The high dosage of medicine caused insomnia. I was not physically strong

129

enough and was still having too much arthritic pain to roam around the house alone, so I would just lay in bed waiting for daybreak to come. Consistent rational thinking was a pleasant change after the high fever I had experienced only weeks ago. My mind would go a hundred miles a minute identifying all the various things I could do to pass the time if only I were better. "If I were better," I would say, "I could do downstairs, call some friends, work on a jigsaw puzzle, read, or watch some TV. If we had a mansion, my aunt and I wouldn't have to share a room, and I could turn the light on to read in bed without disturbing her." *Only if . . .* , I thought; *only if!*

"Well, *if*'s don't count," I reminded myself, staring through the darkness. "I'll just have to wait until morning. It's uncomfortable, but not unbearable." Truly everything is relative; I had experienced enough pain and suffering to know that. However, my real consolation came from hearing the rhythmic breathing of my mom and aunt, as they recaptured the lost nights of sleep that had resulted from the long hospital stay. "I wish I could sleep," I confessed to myself with envy. "But my day will come." And off I went into some mystical fantasy vision of a place in time where I would live a normal life again, sleep and all.

After being home only a few short days, I suddenly found myself faced with yet another new earth-shattering problem. I began having severe physical withdrawal symptoms from the medicine! My body had become accustomed to receiving the very high dosage of steroids intravenously and was in no way willing to change. Although the dosage had been lowered to sixty milligrams a few days prior to my release from the hospital, my body didn't respond right away. Almost like a delayed reaction, it took my body a while to catch on to the change that had transpired. This new response to it all seemed to just jump at me from out of nowhere.

The first day or two back home were a little trying, to say the least. Lying in the bed for such a long period of time really sapped my energy and strength. I thought this to be normal and temporary, but as time went on, things got worse. Each and every night seemed to bring more pain and discomfort. Pretty soon, my entire body began to ache as nausea overwhelmed me. It all reached a peak one morning just before dawn. I rolled out of the bed and crept to the bathroom. Although my muscles were extremely weak and my joints were very stiff, I felt as if I had to move. I just *had* to! I had to go somewhere; I had to do something—I just couldn't lie there in that bed another minute. So I got myself to the bathroom, weak, stiff, and feeling very, very ill. All I could do was call my friend, my mom, for help.

"Maaa-aa-a," I tried to scream. "Maa-aa," I whispered a second time while sitting on the toilet seat, trembling all over, shaking uncontrollably, and gagging. I hadn't eaten; it had been too early for breakfast. Why was I so sick?

Groggy from sleep, Mom towered over my bent-over body and answered my cry. "What's wrong?"

"I don't know," I replied between sobs. "What's wrong with me?" I redirected the same question back to her.

"I don't know." She continued the cyclical dialogue with a puzzled look on her face. "What happened?"

"I was just lying in bed and began to feel real sick. I came in here and started to shake. I feel terrible!" We both knew I had not eaten anything that could have made me sick, since I was not able to go downstairs to the kitchen alone and we didn't have any food upstairs. I hadn't had anything, so what was wrong with me?

"Lets' call the doctor," she suggested. I waited on the toilet, afraid to leave; I knew I couldn't run back had urgency beckoned.

She returned shortly with his presumed diagnosis. "It sounds like withdrawal symptoms from the lowered dosage of steroids. He said you should go back up to eighty milligrams."

"Don't these things ever get tired of making my life difficult?" I respond angrily. Disappointed that this would be the answer, yet relieved that there was an answer, I reluctantly agreed, "OK." Still, I wondered to myself if this merry go round would ever stop.

Mom hurried downstairs to make me a slice of toast—taking the medicine on an empty stomach would have made things worse—and I made my way back to bed, feeling not only terribly sick but unusually strange. I lay in bed thinking, *What a trip! I'm a true to life legal junkie; a real drug addict, and I'm not even high!* I waited for my fix.

That day went by, and so did others. The insomnia continued, and so did the fatigue. Again with prayer and lots of effort, God got me through that, too. A catch twenty-two position, the treatment was necessary to prevent kidney dialysis, to help stop the skin lesions and prevent sepsis, and also prevent other organ involvement—all of which were life-threatening in their own right—but the side-effects were still devastating. It was definitely like choosing the lesser of two evils; a real bummer! Nevertheless, I continued on my path of recuperation.

I would sit for hours on end, just waiting for the sun to rise so the rest of the world would wake up with me. Company was the only thing to which I had to look forward; my activities those days were so limited. They were very similar to those days spent in Ohio. My activities revolved only around sleeping, eating, reading, and possibly watching TV, and even that was a chore. When I wasn't trying to contend with the consistent intense pain, I was dealing with the weakness. I did not understand how my body could feel as if it had been used for a punching bag when I had done absolutely nothing but rested. The overall soreness and stiffness was even more difficult to deal with than the three kinds of arthritis I had each day. Still no sleep and only ten-minute catnaps during the day, sometimes—maybe. I really did long for a normal night's sleep.

As the weeks passed on, things progressed. Soon I was able to bathe myself and go downstairs at least once a day. Of course, it was best if I waited until after lunch because, once down, there was no going back up until bedtime. One trip a day was all I could handle. Again, I thank God for the understanding and support of my family. They always went to whatever lengths necessary to do their best to help me, and these days were no exception.

We never had a lot of money, but thanks to God, our modest needs were always met. Our two-bedroom townhouse did not have a bathroom downstairs, so the worst part of my afternoon was having the use the bedpan so frequently. Thanks to diuretics and hypertensive drugs, I had to go quite a bit. So much for privacy! Still, it was great just being downstairs for a few hours with others in an environment other than the four walls of my bedroom. The love of my family stretched forth again, as my mom and my Aunt Evelyn more than willingly carried the bedpan up and down the stairs too many times to count. They waited on me hand and foot to help me bear the cross that seemed to be all my own. Their love was unending, as they frequently stated how they wished they could have done even more. What a blessing they were! They never seemed to get tired of exercising my body parts to loosen them, getting me dressed and undressed, or the many other mundane duties that I needed help with.

My relationship with my mom grew even more precious. She not only addressed my physical needs, but she caressed my heart when it ached from disappointment or pain; she helped clear my thoughts with wisdom when cumbered with confusion or doubt, and she reassured my self-confidence when uneasiness seemed to creep in. She was definitely a stabilizing force in my life and the lives of many others. My mom was a very sensitive person and an even more responsive mother. We shared a lot; nothing was off limits to us. We were, in essence, best friends. Our relationship was very open, honest, and full of love—a healthy kind of love at that. She was the kind of person that stood for the idea that right is right and wrong is wrong, yet her love for others was unconditional. She may have approved or disapproved of certain actions, but her love would remain the same. Her love was neither to be won nor earned, it just *was*. We both knew that God had graced her to be what and who she was, and we thanked Him daily for the person and the mother He had given us in the personality of her. She's no longer physically here with me, but her strength and love will forever live on in my heart. As time moved on, I begun to gain greater knowledge and understanding of who and what God was. It was during these days that I had an even greater experience with the Spirit of God.

During one of those many sleepless nights, I sat reading the Bible by the night-light. As a matter of fact, I was reading the Gospel of John, where numerous accounts of the many miracles performed by

Christ is recorded. In the middle of my study, I heard the voice of the Lord speak to me. It came as a thought in my mind, but at the same time, it was also audible as if someone else was speaking to me. It was externally audible and internally felt. It touched my spirit, and I *felt* in my heart that the instructions I received were good. Good how? I don't know. It just felt right and OK.

The voice said to me very plainly, "Go downstairs."

Of course I hesitated. "I'm not strong enough to go downstairs by myself," I reasoned with myself and God. It just wasn't a wise thing to do, I thought, cautiously.

Now, I really did know the voice of God, and I knew He was truly the God of the universe; so why then, did I feel this uncontrollable need to dispute the wisdom of His instructions? Only because I knew I did not have enough strength on my own to do this thing, and *I* wanted to be in control. Isn't that usually why we don't exercise our faith in the great Jehovah? I believed God could handle it, at least in my head I did, but what about in my heart? There's a difference, you know. God was now requiring me to prove to Him that I believed—in my heart—that He could. If my heart believed, then I would act, and it would not matter at all what my mind argued. My job was simply to just go, even if I did not know exactly what to expect. I hesitated because I was uncomfortable with the unknown. I knew God was God, but I had never experienced Him on the level that He was now asking me to trust Him.

I was sick; my legs were weak, and my entire body seemed to weigh a ton. I might fall and hurt my fragile body that was already short on functioning. And if I did fall, I probably couldn't yell loud enough for anyone to come to my rescue. I knew I didn't have the physical strength or ability in my limbs to get myself up. "You must be crazy," I said to Him and to myself again, but still it felt right in my spirit for me to follow His instructions to go downstairs, in spite of my fears and my logic.

It simply felt like the right thing to do because it was my Creator talking to me. It was not my limited feeble little mind giving me these instructions, but instead, it was the voice of the force that had created me—that had bought me into mere existence, who knew me before I even knew myself. The Creator of mankind, the Creator of the boisterous winds, the vast oceans, and the huge mountains that we look upon in awe. That powerful force whose understanding, knowledge, and wisdom, supercedes our own in ways incomprehensible to man. In all of our best efforts, man can never understand God in His fullest. So why try to understand? Why try to intellectualize it? Why try to analyze it? It just felt right—plain and simple!

Yet, in my ignorance, I too continued to analyze these instructions to the best of my ability. When all of a sudden, I heard the voice speak again in the same calm, yet authoritative tone, as it commanded, "Go downstairs."

You know, God has never been one of a lot of words. Even when He created this vast intricately detailed world we live in, the Bible says He simply said, "Let there be light." That's awesome, to just speak something into existence!

On this particular morning He must have spoken my actions into existence that very same way, because these instructions were no doubt in total conflict with what I thought, yet I mysteriously put the Bible down and immediately stood on my feet. I turned and proceeded to walk into the hallway, and before I knew what had happened, I found myself downstairs!

It was as if someone had actually carried me down the stairs. For the first time in months, I did not have to stop every few steps to rest, and it seemed I reached the bottom in no time at all. It was as if I had floated down! *Why am I doing this*, I wondered. *Where am I going?* I had no answer to either of these questions.

As my mind raced for answers, I floated along. The gravitation of the force was so strong, I just simply followed. When I finally found myself at a complete stop, I happened to be in the dining room facing our wall clock, which read 7:00 A.M. As soon as the time registered in my brain, I heard the same voice say, *"You are healed."*

I stood there in disbelief, partly because I heard this audible voice but saw no one, and partly because someone or something was dealing with me on an issue that was very much a concern of my heart but not even on my mind at the time.

135

I mean, of course I wanted to be well, but I had been far too busy dealing with day to day issues to concentrate much on it. *This is strange*, I thought, as I continued to stand there mesmerized. Although I was quite sure what had been said to me, I still couldn't quite believe it, so I responded with the question, "What?" In His patience, in His love, and in His mercy, He kindly repeated the same words, *"You are healed!"*

I assume He thought I was ready to handle something like that, since He had been dealing with me spiritually and I had been studying His Word for the past three years. Still, it was a new experience for me to actually talk with God this way. A real trip! The entire experience was simply awesome; even the way I had gotten downstairs was strange. And the calmness I felt during the entire experience was absolutely unbelievable. I felt as if the entire room was flooded with the presence of Almighty God, and an indescribable sort of extreme peace saturated with love encompassed me. There was even an illumination in the room, a hazy bright glow that just kind of filled the entire airspace. The voice I heard was more than real, if you can imagine that. It was more real than anything I had ever heard on earth before. It was as if the voice was inside my heart, in my mind, outside my ears yet entering into my ears, and in every corner of the room, all at the same time. It was absolutely incredible! It was so real that I expected to see Jesus appear in the room at any moment. You see, there was a special knowing that this voice I heard had come from Jesus, the Son of God, and not God the Father. I don't know how to explain it, except to say I just *knew* it. That in itself was a little strange since all of my previous spiritual experiences had involved God or the Holy Spirit. I guess God felt it was now time to personally introduce me to the third person of the Trinity, His Son—how excited and how honored I felt. I now understand that it was the welts and stripes Jesus took upon His body that made my healing possible, so it was only fitting that He would be the one to speak my deliverance to me. In short, what I was experiencing was a miracle! A genuine, authentic miracle, just like the ones recorded in the Holy Scriptures that occurred thousands of years ago.

I soon began to be joyful that my sickness was to be a thing of the past, as the message transmitted from my spirit to my mind; when suddenly the voice came again with further instructions, "Now, go and tell your mother."

I turned and immediately started walking towards the stairs again. Even I was amazed at how obedient I was, but when having a face to face encounter with one's Creator, how can there be a choice?

Miraculously enough, I went upstairs just as easily as I had gone down. As I walked, I found my body feeling like it had before I had ever gotten sick in Cincinnati years before. There was no arthritic pain, and there was no joint pain. The dagger-type chest pains were gone, and so was the heaviness of my body. I even had the control and flexibility of my fingers back.

As I walked up the stairs, God's Holy Spirit quickened my spirit and brought to my remembrance the truths I had read in the Bible during my many times of study. He reminded me that seven was His number, that when He created the world, He rested on the seventh day. When the walls of Jericho fell, Joshua and the people were instructed to march around them seven times. When Naaman was healed of leprosy, he was told to wash in the Jordan River seven times, and there are countless other examples. Seven is God's number! It signifies wholeness; it means completeness, total perfect completeness.

He brought to my attention the experience downstairs and the fact that when I faced the clock, it said seven o'clock! Praise God! The Holy Spirit also quickened to my spirit an account in the Bible wherein Jesus healed ten lepers and told them to go show themselves to the priest, and as they went, they were healed. So, I anxiously went into my mother's room and excitedly proclaimed, "Momma, Jesus told me to tell you that I'm healed!"

She was asleep and mumbled, "OK."

I don't think it registered; I'm not even sure she believed me, but I *knew* in my heart what had happened. I *knew* it was real! I knew what I had experienced, and no one could ever make me doubt that. Once you know that you know, there is no doubt.

There is a definite distinction between *believing* in something and *knowing* something. Beliefs, when tested, can be shattered, swayed, or even changed, but knowledge, true knowledge, can weather any storm and pass any test. Knowledge will stand; real truth never changes.

So as time went on, I confessed my healing to anyone that would listen. I didn't really care what people thought or if they believed me or not. I knew what I had experienced. I also knew about the power of the tongue and how what we say has a strong influence on what transpires in our lives, so I persisted with my truth. I had seen enough evidence of God's Word come alive in my life that I believed in my heart, mind, and soul the words Jesus had spoken to me that morning in our dining room.

I had witnessed a visit from and had spoken with my Creator in a very special way; truly, I had experienced a close encounter with the Absolute, the Great I Am—My God.

I could have very easily stood fast on Holy Scriptures like that of Mark 11:23–24 and believed God for my healing, but I didn't. Although I did and still do have faith in my God for who He is, the healing I received was not based on my faith. My healing was a divine gift from God, freely given that others may see and believe that Jesus Christ is the same yesterday, today, and forevermore! God the Father, God the Son, and God the Holy Ghost is still alive today, still moving in the earth, still going about delivering those in bondage and healing all manner of sickness and diseases. Won't you give Him a try today? Ask Jesus to come into your heart.

7. The Extant End

The scars are fading nicely now. The marks that so often remind me of the rawness of my skin that used to plague my daily life with pain and inconvenience can barely be seen. I am no longer forced to use the variety of creams and ointments two, three, or four times a day. Money previously used for those and other medicines can now be used for other things. These days I can use baby oil or lotion to lubricate my dry skin, as do most other normal people. I use cocoa butter or vitamin E oil to assist nature in fading the blemishes, but that, too, is an option, not a necessity. My scalp sometimes itches, but not because of scaling patches or sores. It now itches because of hair bumps generating new hair growth in places that were once completely bald. The medical profession in numerous states around the country frequently made negative prognoses of doom and gloom in regards to my case. They said the cells in my scalp were dead; thus, the hair follicles would never generate hair again—but my God is a God of change. He creates where there is nothing, and He gives life to that which is dead. So, now I have hair growing back on that very same scalp that was the focus of such negative, hopeless reports.

Time assists miraculously in any healing process, whether physically, mentally, emotionally, or spiritually. Although God can and does sometime heal instantaneously, the element of time allows the manifestation of nature's true perfection to take place in its fullness. Time is the one essential element needed for the ingrained processes of nature to unfold. It is only through time that nature's intrinsic activities can take place and yield its true character.

The many hospital visits, the numerous needles, and blood tests are all memories of a time that once was. I no longer take

nitroglycerin, Tagament, Zantac, Placquenil, Atabrine, hydro-
chlorothiazide, nor any of the other fourteen prescription drugs
that were once not only a ritual in my daily life, but also necessary
for my survival. I often reflect back, as my mind's eye briefly pro-
jects sketches of the laborious, difficult, and yes, painful episodes of
my life, and I thank my God.

I thank God for giving me the strength, courage, and patience
to endure those times. I can in no way take the credit nor the glory
for being able to stand through such horrendous storms in my life.
It was only through the help of Almighty God that I was able to
endure. I needed a power greater than my own to survive such trauma, and I found it in God. I thank God for being real in my life and
not being some mystical fantasy. I had been taught that God was
high up in the heavens looking down here on earth. Well, that may
be true, but I've also found it to be true that God is right here on
earth with me—living, breathing, and moving in my midst. I am so
grateful that He is alive and well—that He not only is the God of
the Bible but He is also the God of today, in this world, and even
in my life. I thank God that the words I read in the Holy Scriptures
are real enough to come to life to the point of manifestation here
in this physical realm when believed and received by the reader or
the hearer.

I thank God for moving in and through the many circumstances and situations that confronted me. Time and time again,
I witnessed the invisible hand of God move to make, to create, to
change, or even to eradicate, the many situations in my life. He
would and still does use whatever or whosoever necessary to work
out the situations or circumstances for my good. He will even use
the negative situations to protect, to provide for, and to sometimes even raise up His people. He did it in the biblical days with
Joseph in Egypt; He did it for Shadrach, Meshach, and
Abednego. He did it for Daniel in the lions' den; He did it for
Rehab, and He did it for me. He worked through people I knew
and people I didn't know, people that knew and served Him and
people that didn't. He worked through them all just to bring
about that which was good for me in my life.

I thank God for working through the doctors, the nurses, and the many other medical personnel that He blessed me with. He gave them wisdom, knowledge, and understanding. He graced them with skill, technology, and equipment. He even gave them brilliant minds, strong, determined wills, and hearts full of compassion—all of which benefited me. God even supplied me with the best, and yes, sometimes the most expensive medical care available in a time when healthcare was a major concern for most Americans. Good healthcare was not always the norm for all people, but my God saw fit to make it available, accessible, and possible for me to have. Truly my God is my Jehovah Jireh! The Lord is my provider!

I also thank God for the awesome love and support of my family and friends. So many times they could have gotten tired and walked away, but they didn't. They just kept on hanging in there with me. Even when times got so bleak that there was absolutely no light in sight, my family continued to give all they had. When that wasn't enough they, too, would pull on God, who was their power source, and got more. They let me know that their love for me was unending, and there was nothing that they wouldn't do for me, nothing was too much for them. They stayed up nights, slept in hospital chairs, missed enormous amounts of time from work, and whatever else they needed to do to help me with my fight. Nothing was too hard for them. I appreciate that!

During the years of my illness, their lives became a roller coaster along with mine. They, like me, weren't sure what to expect from one minute to the next. The unpredictable nature of lupus complicated their lives, in some ways, even more so than it did mine. At least I was in direct communication with my body and its limitations; they weren't. They dealt blindly in a lot of instances. Nevertheless, their love for me continued to abound. They stayed by my side and were always willing to flow with the currents of my life.

My friends were pretty much the same way. They were always there for me. If in the same physical perimeter, they would visit. If not close by, they would call and send cards or flowers, whatever they could to let me know that they were with me, in spirit, and that they loved me. However, their support was not only emotional—a true issue of the heart—but their support was also sometimes financial. There were many times I would receive a check in the mail or a phone call asking if I needed anything. They knew I was not working and needed help. You see, I was one of those people whose financial status allowed me to fall through the cracks of our society. My Fortune 500 company paid me too much disability income for state or local assistance, but not enough to maintain a normal comfortable lifestyle. I was one of those who had too much to be classified as *poor* and too little to be classified as anything else. Some didn't understand because they felt they were struggling, too, but the difference was, their incomes increased with the cost of living; mine didn't. They were struggling because they continued to increase their spending along with the increase of income, so they felt they were never getting ahead. But my struggle was simply trying to maintain what I had. I didn't want to go backwards, but then again, who does? So, my friends would step in and pick up where my family and I were forced to leave off. Once, when things were really bad and my prescription bills were an exorbitant amount, some of my sorority sisters united funds and cabled me money by surprise. My church family was the same way—always there ready to help. I thank God for touching their hearts to the point that they were willing to share what they had with me. Even when I could no longer compete in the societal roles, nor flow in the social circles that were expected of me after attending such a prestigious college, my friends still accepted me for what and where I was; they never shunned me. So many times they would leave where they were and come to me where I was—physically, mentally and emotionally. They were always a very strong system of support for me. I thank God for my friends and my family. No one could have had better.

Although I am extremely grateful to God for all of these things, I am most grateful to Him for giving me the opportunity to share this testimony and story with those of you who may not know that the God we all hear and read about as children is alive and real today!

My life has now changed so drastically. I can now walk for miles, if I so desire. I can run; I can chase in play. I can squat, and I can even sit on the floor, if I so desire. And that's the real blessing, having the choice to do so. Rising out of a chair is a snap, and so is sitting down in one. But it hasn't always been that way. There are no more uncertainties as to whether I will shower tomorrow or not, at least not uncertainties in the extreme sense of the word. Now I shower subconsciously, concentrating on the task before me when I finish, instead of the effort I'm putting forth to get the job done.

I once again have the pleasure of reading without my vision being blurred, and I can snap my fingers to my favorite tunes. I have the flexibility in my fingers and the dexterity of my muscles to pick up a fork or hold a pen and the strength necessary to push that pen across the paper to write.

I can now balance myself to walk downstairs without holding the side rails; I can even run down, if I so desire. I can balance myself on the toilet seat enough to reach for the tissue, even if it isn't directly in front of me. Oh, how blessed I am!

I can file and polish my nails and even get my feet in the chair to do my toenails. I can drive my car and carry my own purse, even if it's filled with everything but the kitchen sink. I can carry my own groceries to the car and in the house when I go to the supermarket. I can even open the big heavy doors in public buildings all by myself and not have to wait for someone else to come along to help! These are all activities I do subconsciously now, but I never take them for granted. You see, these are very special blessings; God in His infinite sovereignty could command our body parts to stop functioning at any time. He and He alone is the Creator that gives life to our lifeless and otherwise dead bodies. You see, man in his great technologically advanced and mentally competent world cannot even breath on his own. Man cannot cause or stop his brain from sending appropriate signal to other parts of his body—only God can. Now, we have genetic engineering and in vitro fertilization and all other kinds of scientific exploitations that enable us to play at being God, but the bottom line is that, whatever man does, he is only tampering with an already established existence. The first and initial existence is always the greatest—so it is with God, the Creator of our universe. He is the first, and He is the greatest; everything else is only secondary and subservient.

I proclaim to you today that the Creator of mankind is the Creator of this great universe, and nothing can exist without Him. He is the creative force that founded the heavens and established the earth. "All things were made by Him and without Him was not anything made that was made" (Saint John 1:3). He is the Creator of my life and all life upon the face of this earth. He is the God of all gods and the Lord of all lords.

He is the great I Am. That means He is so very awesome and powerful that He can and will be anything and all things that we may need or want Him to be. In essence, He is saying, "I am _____ ." You fill in the blank!

God is all powerful, and Jesus does heal. He healed my body, and now I can say, "He had a cure when no man did."

He healed my mind and lifted it to higher levels of understanding, knowledge, wisdom, and will. He transformed my way of thinking. He elevated my way of thinking. My mind has been reoriented—I am no longer bound by societal conditioning. I now know and understand that I do not have to be a mental slave to the ways and cares of this world, nor to the lust of my fleshly nature, but I can rise above it all. My mind has been liberated, and I have been set *free*! This freedom can only come through Jesus the Christ.

Most of all He healed my spirit. I have been redeemed and made one with Him. It is only through this rebirth and regeneration of spirit that all else is possible. Being born again is the answer. It is the *only* thing that makes sense out of this thing called life. God's Spirit touching our spirit—manifesting His Son and His purpose in our lives—that's the only way to true peace and real happiness. That, in essence, is life!

Now that the episode with lupus is over, I depend very heavily on my spirit in every facet of my life. I depend on it to guide and direct me in where to live, when to move, where to move, and practically everything else I to do. I depend on it to guide me on how to budget my money, where to shop, what to buy, what to wear, and even sometimes what to eat. God says in His Word that, if we acknowledge Him in all our ways, He will direct our paths. That means, even when we think things are minor, God is still interested.

Nevertheless, my spirit can only be trusted with such important decisions if, and only if, it is one with the Spirit of God. Only when I—my spirit—am connected with the Spirit of my maker can I receive the kind of guidance necessary to make such wise and correct decisions. I must reach out in a spiritual way.

Some may ask, "How do I get in touch with my spirit?" The key is not to get in touch with *your* spirit, but to get in touch with God. Because our spirits are the only pure part of us that is capable of making direct contact with God, sincere communication with God inevitably leads to life for our spirit-man; it will, in essence, come alive. Although we may not always understand exactly how or what it is happening, there is definitely a knowing on the inside that true communication is taking place and that a significant change is occurring within us. Once communication with God begins, then knowledge and understanding of one's spiritual nature can take place.

Nevertheless, the part of us that we can best judge to be our spirits prior to being regenerated with the mind of Christ is our hearts. Our hearts are the main things that God deals with. A pure heart is the *only* thing that God requires to introduce Himself to us. Once we open up our hearts to Him, He will in no doubt come in.

The situation I had with lupus just happens to be the vehicle He used to show Himself strong and mighty in my life. Your situation may be similar, or your situation may be different. Whatever the case, God is still God, and He is still ready and willing to be a part of your life. Won't you invite Him into your heart and life today? It's very simple! If you have not been living a life that is pleasing to God or obedient to His Word, all you have to do is repent and ask Him to forgive you. Receive His son, Jesus the Christ, as that method by which God has provided to reconcile you back to Him, and He will come to live in your heart. The results will be great. You will then have eternal life and a much more abundant life here on earth.

Of all the lessons I've learned in life, the greatest by far has been the importance of my spirit being connected with the Spirit of Almighty God.

Acknowledgements

Special thanks to Kevin and Steve for the use of their office equipment. To Cynthia, the whiz kid, for sacrificing her time and expertise. To Mike and Barbara for their faith and support of my work. To Helema for suggesting the valuable luncheon that opened the right door to getting this book published.

About the Author

Susan L. Majette grew up in the Tidewater area of Virginia. Educated in the public school system, she went on to receive her bachelor's degree from Hampton University in Hampton, Virginia. Her work experiences include employment in the private sector, as well as teaching in a public school system and working as a student psychiatric social worker.

At the age of twenty-three, Ms. Majette was diagnosed with systemic lupus erythematosus, only nine months after she had graduated from college. "It was an earth shattering experience," she says, "to be diagnosed with an incurable disease after being healthy all of my life. Nevertheless, with the help of the Lord, I found a way to learn and grow from the experience, using the stumbling blocks as stepping stones. This brings me to the point I am today, with a story to tell and a life of hope to share."

In learning to cope with lupus, Ms. Majette focused her energies on researching the disease that had taken over her life. This research yielded information and knowledge that was the basis for the establishment of the Peninsula Lupus Support Group in 1982, later chartered as the Peninsula Chapter of the National Lupus Foundation of America. She is now very active in ministry, bringing about the reality of God's Kingdom on earth, sharing a message of hope with all who will hear.